Glimpses of Jewish Baltimore

Gilbert Sandler

Edited and with a foreword by Avi Y. Decter

The History Press

The Jewish Museum of Maryland
at the Herbert Bearman Campus

Published by The History Press
Charleston, SC 29403
www.historypress.net

Co-published by the Jewish Museum of Maryland, Inc.
Baltimore, MD 21202
www.jewishmuseummd.org

Front cover, color image: Untitled, by Jacob Glushakow, n.d. Gift of Samuel and Naomi Boltansky, 2010.83.4.

First published 2012

Manufactured in the United States

ISBN 978.1.60949.653.1

Library of Congress CIP data applied for.

Contents

CONTENTS

Foreword

We live by stories," Elie Wiesel has remarked. And the master teller of Baltimore Jewish stories is Gilbert Sandler. As a close observer of Baltimore Jewry, Gil Sandler has no peer. A native Baltimorean, he has been living its history for eight decades and writing about it for nearly as long (or so it seems). For more than thirty years, his "Baltimore Glimpses" appeared weekly in the *Baltimore Sun*, and his monthly columns on Baltimore Jewish history were published for almost fifteen years in the *Baltimore Jewish Times*. He has also served as an editor and contributor to *Generations*, the annual journal of the Jewish Museum of Maryland. Gil has published three bestselling volumes with Johns Hopkins University Press—*Jewish Baltimore, Small Town Baltimore* and *Home Front Baltimore*—and now he is the narrator of a weekly public radio series, *Baltimore Stories*, on WYPR.

This collection of stories about Jewish Baltimore focuses on everyday life from the 1920s through the 1980s, touching on good days and hard times, coming of age and growing old. Each narrative is tinged with nostalgia, but also with insight, empathy and wit. Gil Sandler's Baltimore is a world of vivid scenes, lively characters and a chorus of vibrant voices. Riding the streetcars, playing sandlot softball, demonstrating for civil rights, coping with the Great Depression—all are recalled in crisp, compelling prose.

Gil's stories evoke what he calls "the tumble of life." One of the many strengths of his prose is his ability to call out the exemplary instance, the telling detail, the resonant quote. This is coupled with a wonderful instinct for "finding the story." Some of the topics Gil addresses are typical—stories of family business or ethnic foodways or religious education. But others are unexpected: a Jewish agricultural colony, or a summer camp for impoverished youth or the changed character of a beloved neighborhood.

Each tale reprinted here is informative and enjoyable; collectively, they tell a story of an ethnic community getting comfortable in America. The stories in this volume sketch Baltimore Jews as they integrated into the larger community. Mass migration of Jews from Eastern Europe ended in 1924, and these narratives reveal the first and second and third generations maintaining their Jewish identities while becoming fully American.

This selection of Gil Sandler's essays is published with deep appreciation to Andrew Buerger, publisher of the *Baltimore Jewish Times*, and to two *Jewish Times* editors, Neil Rubin and Alan Feiler. In 2009, Gil donated all of his *Jewish Times* columns to the Jewish Museum of Maryland, which is proud to co-sponsor this volume. Special thanks to Dr. Deborah R. Weiner, research historian at the Museum; to Harold Steinly-Marks, who assisted in organizing the Sandler typescripts; to Rachel Kassman, the Museum's photo archivist; to Amy Smith, the Museum's administrative coordinator; and to collections interns Mary Dwan and Emilie Reed. Special thanks to Efrem Potts for his careful edits. Thanks also to Hannah Cassilly, Darcy Mahan and the production team at The History Press for their many contributions to this book. Most credit is due, of course, to Gil Sandler, whose generosity, insight and sparkling writing bring to life the coming of age of an American Jewish community.

Avi Y. Decter, Jewish Museum of Maryland

AUTHOR'S NOTE: In preparing this text for publication, strenuous effort was exerted to ensure the accuracy and consistency of proper names. However, over a century's time, names change and variant spellings creep in. If any error has been made, please inform the Jewish Museum of Maryland so that any errors can be revised in future printings.

PART 1

Creating Community

For more than a century, from the 1820s into the 1940s, East Baltimore was *the* Jewish neighborhood, the Lower East Side of Baltimore. Here was the vibrant center of immigrant Jewish life. Decade after decade, newcomers moved in, looking to get by and then to get ahead. And, decade by decade, they moved out and up, following a northwest line of mobility and migration that led from Eutaw Place out Park Heights Avenue and on to Pikesville, Owings Mills and beyond.

There were other Jewish neighborhoods that lay beyond the main line of northwest movement, but these were outliers—clusters of residents in West Baltimore and pockets of Jewish settlement in neighborhoods to the south, as well. There were also some remarkable anomalies: the country estates of the very wealthy and even a Jewish agricultural colony. The voices in these neighborhood stories are distinct, each in its own way. Together they constitute a medley of memory, inflected with a mix of vibrancy and nostalgia.

Baltimore's Lost Colony

Few among the motorists streaking by Beltway Exit 16 at seventy miles per hour, passing close to Security Boulevard and Johnnycake Road, appreciate the significance of that tiny piece of geography. But just after the turn of the century, in the early 1900s, the area supported the ghost farm of Ya'azor, the lost Jewish agricultural colony in Baltimore.

Beginning in 1906, around nineteen Jewish families moved into the barren farm country with high hopes and the sense of escape, aspiring to an American-Jewish experience free of the ghetto life of East Baltimore. They would be farmers, owning the land and living off its rich harvest, independent of union bosses and sweatshops. But the dream would die.

> *I, Isaac Rodbell, at the request of Dr. Aberbach* [of the Baltimore Hebrew College] *on this 3 January 1975 have been asked to give information in regard to the establishment of the Jewish colony, about 1905 in Baltimore County on Johnnycake Road about nine miles west of the city line. The settlement received a charter under the name of Ya'azor, which means "God will help." It would consist of fifteen* [sic] *families. We moved there in 1906. I was seven years old.*
>
> *I remember some of the families who moved into the colony at about the same time and on similar acreage: Abraham Weinstein, his wife, two sons, two daughters. Tobias Goodman and his wife—they had no children. Jacob Kramer, wife, daughter, three sons. Plotkin, two sons and a daughter. Gelman, wife and three children. Goldstein, wife and children. Finkelstein, wife, no children. Wolf Kalinsky, no children.*

In the late 1880s, Jewish activist, millionaire and philanthropist Baron Maurice de Hirsch concluded sadly that the best hope for East European Jews' survival and freedom was agricultural colonization. To that end, he allocated $2 million to establish Jewish agricultural colonies in America (and in Argentina and other countries as well). Ya'azor in Baltimore was one of the agricultural communities brought into being by the Baron de Hirsch Fund.

The beginnings of Ya'azor in Baltimore (also known as "Yiddishe Colona" and "Jew Town") go back to the founding family of the Joseph Weinsteins. In 1980, Mrs. Joseph "Rose" Weinstein told *Jewish Times* writer Janice Levitt, "My husband, Joseph, took his brother and their father looking all over Baltimore for a site. They had little money and so it was not easy to find enough land to make a colony of families. And they wanted a site not too far from the city. Finally a plot of land was registered for 351 acres to nine individuals under the name of 'Ya'azor.'" With financing from the Baron de Hirsch Fund, Baltimore's Jewish farming community was born.

Ya'azor was never conceived to be a kibbutz, a model of an Israeli cooperative. Each farmer purchased his own land independently through loans from the Baron de Hirsch Fund and built his own home. Photographs

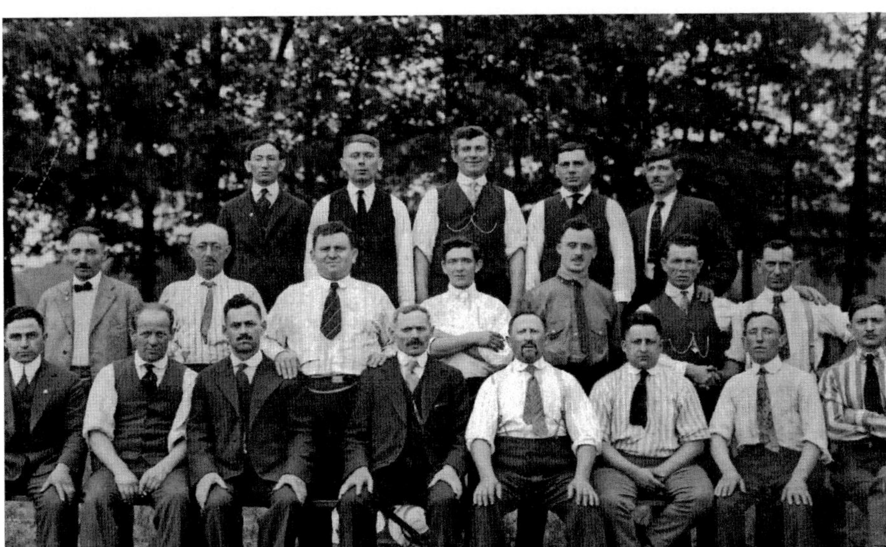

Men like Joseph Walpert (top right) and the others pictured here struggled to adapt to an agrarian lifestyle, with little or no formal training, no electricity and often no running water, circa 1915. The Ya'azor colony did not survive beyond the first generation. *Gift of Mannes F. Greenberg, 1993.28.1.*

show houses that are spare and primitive. Rose Weinstein told of having to take care of the land, the house and the animals: "Twice a week we had the additional chore of going to the city to sell our dairy products, a tedious all-day trip by horse and wagon. We roasted in the summer, we froze in the winter." Another resident recalled that they had no indoor plumbing until 1916.

It was inevitable that the settlers would build a shul. Recollections of it are of a one-room structure, complete with an upstairs balcony for women. Edith Weinstein Brenner recalled, "The young and the elderly walked to it through the woods during the heat of the summer and, in winter, through the snow. At holiday time every seat in the house was taken. I observed services in that shul for thirty years." The synagogue ultimately burned down and was never replaced.

Isaac Rodbell recalled the schooling he received: "We children of Ya'azor farmers walked to a one-room school about a mile and a half away on Johnnycake Road near Rolling Road. The school had about thirty students. There were about six of us from the farm scattered over several elementary school grades." Ann Rodbell Fleisher recalled, "It was heated by a pot-bellied stove. In addition to the usual subjects, reading, writing and arithmetic, the boys were taught farming and the girls the arts of cooking and canning."

Not all of the residents recall life at Ya'azor as harsh, especially those in families that moved to the community in later years, beginning in 1929. David Levin explained why their experience was not all that bad, and

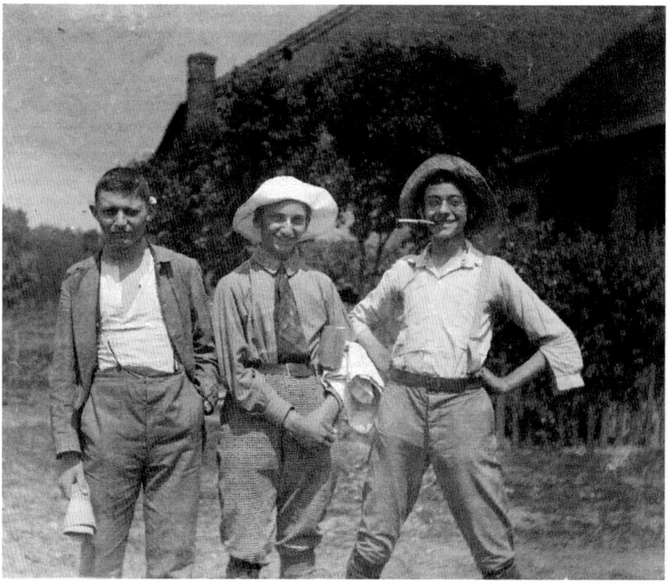

Boys on a farm, circa 1917. *Gift of Max Amichai Heppner, 1995.105.67.*

sometimes joyous: "Tractors replaced the work animals and trucks the horses and buggy. Farming became a lot easier. These advances, along with running water and electric lights made life at the colony more pleasant. We even had a social hall for parties and dancing. My sister Esther played piano, a man named Schaefer played mandolin. But we were only there for about five years."

Overall, in terms of creating a flourishing and productive Jewish community as de Hirsch envisioned, Ya'azor, although free of tenement and sweatshop, was a failure. In retrospect, how could it not be? The settlers were tailors and silversmiths for the most part; they had no experience with farming the land or marketing its products. Some complained of lack of leadership; others, of insufficient capital to support the business end of things. In time and out of necessity, many of the men sought other means of providing for their families—living on the farm but working in Baltimore City as bakers, plumbers, carpenters and tailors. Some of the farmers opened their houses for tourists; others began bootlegging

Isaac Rodbell summed up his view of the Ya'azor experience:

> *In reflection, I look back and I wonder why those Jewish families moved there in the first place. What was the purpose? There was never any cooperation among the families. Nor was there leadership. It always seemed to me that it was every man for himself. Except for a few bright moments, life was bleak. Some of the farms were on the public roads but the majority were not, and ingress and egress in winter and spring because of snow and ice and mud made getting to and from the main road a hardship. To recall life at Ya'azor is very agonizing for me. A painful realization of wasted lives. In my estimation, Ya'azor should go down in Baltimore history as a great tragedy. Inevitably, the children saw the tragedy, and as soon as they could, they got out and moved to the city. The colony began to deteriorate. The young left. The old just died there.*

Speeding by Exit 16, it's hard to know that it was there at all, that it ever happened—this vanished dream called Ya'azor, this lost colony of Baltimore Jewry.

The author is indebted to Ms. Janice Levitt, from whose earlier research on the Ya'azor community I have borrowed generously.

Originally published as "Lost Colony," May 24, 2002.

Halcyon Days at Easterwood Park

If you didn't play softball, it could get lonely." There is a good reason for that view and for the intensity of it, too. Hear Leonard "Lenny" Miller tell it, speaking in the 1980s:

> *I was born at 2200 Pulaski Street. Along with most of the kids, I went to PS 62 on Smallwood Street and then to Garrison Junior High. But every day, all day in the summer, and in winter after school, from the time we were five and six years old, we were in Easterwood Park—playing softball. The only exception for the boys were the years leading up to bar mitzvah, but, save for those few years, the focus of our lives was Easterwood Park, and softball.*
>
> *One of the first things my father bought me—and we did not have any extra money lying around—was a bicycle so that I could bike my way over and back to Easterwood Park more easily. In those neighborhoods, if a boy couldn't play softball, well, he led a lonely life.*

The Jewish families that settled into these row-house blocks were a part of the emigration from Eastern Europe that flowed through Baltimore's Locust Point beginning in the 1880s. They settled in East Baltimore and then, "moving up" by moving out, bought houses with porches and backyards (with lawns) and access to the area parks—Easterwood being the favorite. In these same neighborhoods, they opened "ma and pa" grocery stores, butcher and tailor shops and delis.

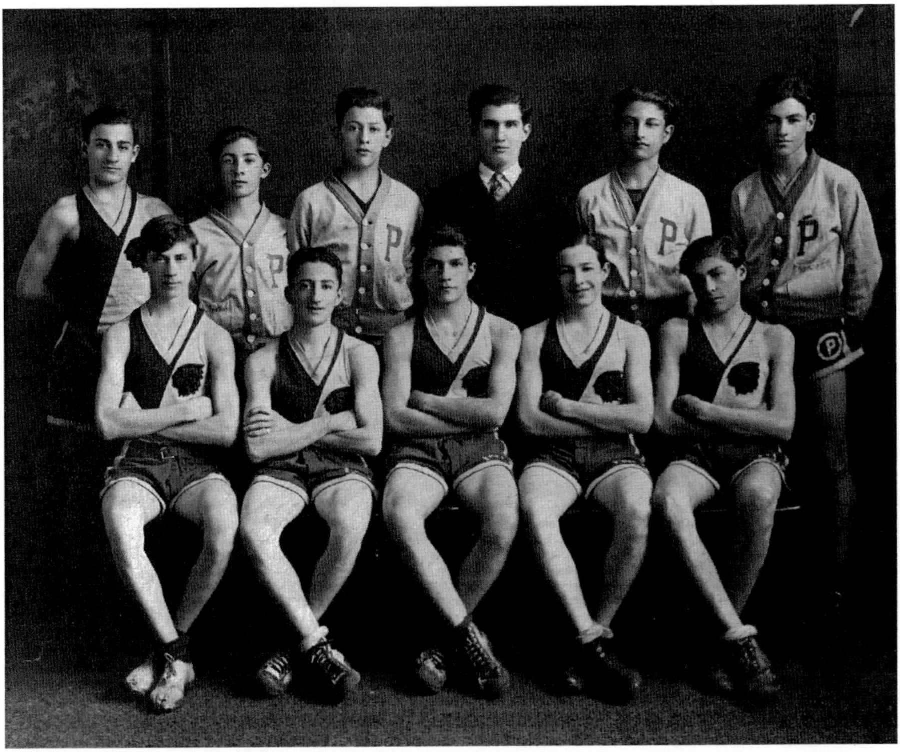

Softball fields weren't all Easterwood Park had to offer. The park also had two basketball courts and two tennis courts. Seen here, proudly boasting their uniforms, is the 1925 Easterwood Park basketball team. *Gift of Rebecca C. Baer, 1997.80.5.*

William "Billy" Lewis lived for all practical purposes at two addresses in the neighborhood: 1802 North Appleton Street, where he was born and slept, and Easterwood Park, where he spent his life on the softball fields

> *since the day I could lift a bat and throw a ball. The park was maybe two blocks long and wide. Besides the three diamonds, it had two basketball courts, two tennis courts and a wooden shingle house that served as an office and storage area for equipment. We took athletics seriously. So seriously, that several of the guys never got over it, and went on to lead professional lives in athletics—Charles Hirschauer, who became coach at Forest Park; Maurice Jacobs, who played for the Kansas City Royals; Lefty Blades, who played for the Detroit Tigers.*

Bill Lewis himself went on to become a physical education director and coach at three Baltimore City high schools.

> *We were seven and eight when we started walking over to the park. There were always attendants on duty to watch you and help you—Mrs. Waxman, Irv Luckman, "Dutch" Baer.*
>
> *We did take time out for lunch. We would go over to Levitt's grocery store, on the corner of Ruxton Avenue and Baker Streets. Mr. Levitt served what was probably the world's first submarine sandwich. He would take a loaf of Pariser's long rye, slit it open long-ways, and slap into it whatever sandwich meats he had at the time. That sub and a bottle of High Rock ginger ale would make lunch for five of us.*

Phil Sherman, who lived at 2106 Rupp Street, was a regular at the park from the time he was five or six years old, and he later became the park's historian. "Hebrew school," he says, "in the year or so leading up to bar

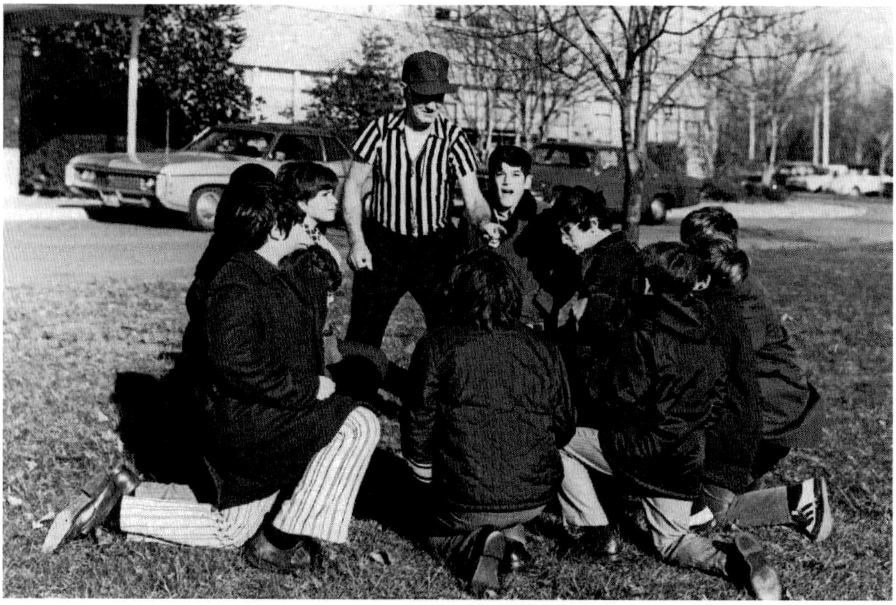

David "Dutch" Baer was a man who loved sports. Director of the Playground Athletic League in the 1930s, Baer was such a sports fan that he and his new bride, Rebecca, spent their honeymoon in Philadelphia watching the basketball team Dutch coached. Here, Baer delivers words of wisdom to young softball players in his beloved Easterwood Park. *Gift of Rebecca C. Baer, 1999.19.13.*

mitzvah, was the only recognized reason why a kid was not over at the park playing softball." He has the records, and he knows the names—"but mostly of the boys. I can't remember many girls."

But Shirley Ballow Rutkowitz, who lived at 2020 Bentalou Street, does. "We went over to the park often. We played beanbag, jacks and jump rope. Girls didn't go to Hebrew school back then, so we had more free time than some of the boys. I recall Shirley Schoenfeld, Annette Brotman Blank, Shirley Berlin, Enid Fritz, and Betty Feldman, Alice Goldstein, Slova Gisner." Bill Lewis adds, "And don't forget Dorothy Greenberg. She was marble champion, year after year. None of the guys could beat her. I know I couldn't." Shirley's husband, Stanley, who lived at 2120 Pulaski Street, adds, "We had one girl in our Hebrew class, Ada Rhea Cohen."

The 2000 and 2001 blocks of West North Avenue made up the commercial center of the neighborhoods: 2000, Weltner's Pharmacy; 2103, Bridges' Deli; 2109, Calvert Five-and-Ten; 2131, Saler's Dairy; 2115, Ballow's; 2117, Holzman's Bakery; 2119, Surasky's butcher shop; 2121, Dr. Ben Sarubin; 2141, Sollod's Pharmacy; and 2217, branch seventeen of the Pratt Library.

Three synagogues served the neighborhoods; the oldest and largest was Har Zion at 2014–16 West North Avenue. Its Hebrew school, which for a boy in those neighborhoods stood ominously between him and playing ball, adjoined. According to Phil Sherman, "Louis Setlin was the congregation's president for many years. Cantor Altman, who lived in Philadelphia, commuted to Baltimore each Friday, and over the Sabbath stayed at the home of Jack, Frank and Bob Levy on Rupp Street." The Hebrew schoolteachers most remembered include Morris Rubin, "Mrs. Goldfarb," "Mr. Schlaffer" and Kopel Weinstein, who became the principal.

Another choice was Tifereth Israel Anshe Sphard. Hillel Mihaly was the rabbi, and attending families included the Alpersteins, Kermishes, Ladons, Rices and Sugarmans. Another option was the Chofetz Chaim, at 2002 Presbury Street, founded by Rabbi Mordechai Rabinowitz. There was even a fourth choice—Schantze's Hall, above the Schantze's movies, for the High Holy Day services only, at North and Pennsylvania Avenues. "Services were conducted," Phil Sherman says, "by Nathan Snyder, a tailor who lived at 2102 Presstman Street, his brother [*sic*] Mendel Rodner, who had a butcher shop in the 2000 block of Westwood Avenue, and his two sons, Abe and Sam."

But always, on the street corners, at the dinner table, in the air, some say in the water, was the sense that the epicenter of life in those neighborhoods was Easterwood Park—watching a game in it, talking about it and, when one got too old for all of that, telling stories about it, remembering it at countless reunions and talking about the sons who came off of those gritty sandlots—judges and doctors and teachers and writers and businessmen—not to recall who made a fortune, who won a coveted award, who was being honored by the community, but who flied out with the bases loaded.

Originally published as "Halcyon Days," August 26, 2005.

Landmark Occasion: Lower Park Heights Comes into Its Own

According to official documents, many of the neighborhoods of Lower Park Heights that most Jewish families moved out of by the 1960s—including Cottage, Keyworth, Shirley and Ulman—are being nominated for inclusion in the prestigious National Register of Historic Places. Those of us who grew up on those streets—sat on those steps, hung out on those corners, walked to the shuls—look in wonderment at this newfound respect for the era and to those old times and places of the heart. Who knew?

The nomination by the Baltimore City Department of Planning to the U.S. Department of the Interior is based on, according to Fred B. Shoken, a city planner, two historic aspects of the neighborhoods: the houses, which were cited as excellent examples of Baltimore housing of the era, and the lifestyle of the neighborhoods as they came together to form "a representative suburban East European Jewish community."

But if you are among those of us who lived in this district (I was born and raised at 3608 Cottage Avenue) and thinking of getting rich by buying back your old house, hold it right there. The inclusion, while prestigious, may not be what you had in mind. Fact is, should the houses and the neighborhoods make it into the National Register, the houses (besides being protected from demolition) become eligible for tax incentives designed to stimulate renovation and rehabilitation. So here's your windfall: you get to rehab your old house at bargain rates.

As for the houses themselves, in its nomination the Baltimore City Commission for Historical and Architectural Preservation (CHAP) waxes rhapsodic, referring to the houses as "architecturally significant." It asserts, for example, "the historic architecture in the houses around Park Circle features a level of design and craftsmanship not found in contemporary housing." Funny, I passed those houses every day of my life until I was eighteen, and you could have fooled me.

The nomination savors the brick duplexes built along Park Heights: "The roofline fronts of these duplexes display a variety of decoration. Fairly simple cornices [3806–12 Park Heights], arched cornice above projecting bays [3908–10 Reisterstown Road], pediments above projecting bays [3709–11 Park Heights] and elaborate curved rooftops [3805–07 Park Heights]—all of which make up the largest grouping of early twentieth-century duplexes in Maryland."

Eight of the twelve blocks facing along Park Heights from Park Circle to Shirley Avenue are composed exclusively of duplexes. We boys in those years, hanging out on the corner of Ulman and Park Heights, known as "Sussman's Corner," seemed hopelessly unaware of our riches.

As for the so-called way of life in the neighborhoods, the nomination suggests that "major historic institutional buildings located within the district boundaries" gave tone and meaning to the residents' lives. "These buildings provided educational and religious services to area residents." To say the least!

"The elementary school that served the neighborhoods was Louisa May Alcott, PS 59," the nomination states. "Constructed in 1910, it is a three-and-a-half- to four-story stucco building with distinctive brick bands, and features large arched dormers and cupolas along a hipped roof and terra cotta decorations." But for all of the data's relevance, they are irrelevant to the memory of school No. 59. "Dormers" are not the stuff of memory. What *is* is the janitor, the gruff Mr. Moore; the white-haired and kindly administrator, Mr. Hayes; and the awesome, all-powerful principal, Mrs. Thalheimer. But I forgive the Department of Planning. How could it know?

"Enoch Pratt Free Library Branch No. 16," the nomination notes, "is a one-story brick building featuring a central pediment and a hipped roof. The projecting entrance bay with limestone decorative door surround is flanked by three windows on either side separated by brick columns and stone bases." More: "The Shaarei Zion synagogue is a stone neo-Greek style building. Walls featuring four ionic columns supporting a central pediment depicting a Ten Commandment motif." The synagogue's Rabbi Tabak should be alive to see such a dismissive description of this centerpiece of his Lower Park Heights empire; he would not be happy. And as for the Talmudical Academy—merely "a Jewish day school at 3701 Cottage Avenue. The yellow brick two-story building with stone entrance bay features stone band courses, glass block at the entrance and Star of David decorations."

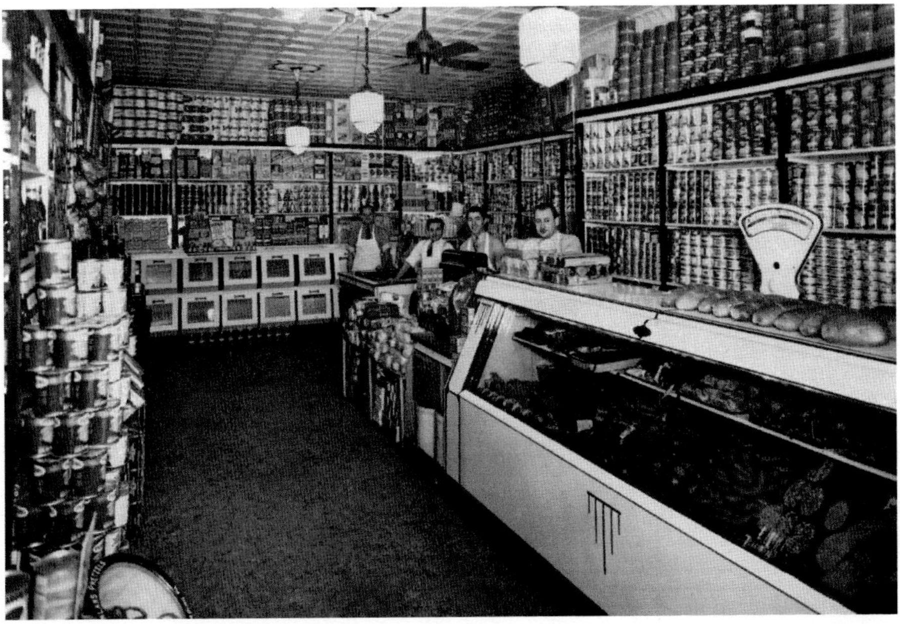

The Joseph Lozinsky Deli and Grocery was where many Park Heights residents went to fill their larders and pantries. *Left to right:* Al Caplan, Joseph Lozinsky, Morris Freiner and Sam Weinstein, pictured standing behind the counter in this 1937 photograph. *Gift of Pauline Weinstein, 1999.35.1.*

The nomination also notes that the "3600 block Cottage Avenue features a bend connecting to Ulman Avenue." That reference to a "bend" doesn't tell the story by half: it was a hard, ninety-degree angle, impossible for most of us sledders to make our Flexible Flyers negotiate the turn, and most of us wound up in a snow bank high on the Kolodners' sidewalk. Some "bend."

Mention is made of the east side of the 3500 block of Park Heights Avenue, the neighborhoods' shopping center of the era: Holzman's bakery, Isaac Davis shoe repair, Lubman's and Thomas butchers, David Schwartz produce and Morris Brenner butter and eggs. Not mentioned (but should be): Joe Lozinsky groceries, Krastman hardware, Blinchikoff confectionery and Tarlow furs. Also not mentioned: several *shochets* (chicken *kasherers*) who operated in garages—with feathers flying.

The nomination notes, too, the prominence in the neighborhood of the Trenton Democratic Club at 3701 Park Heights Avenue (across the street from Kessler's deli) and the civic center of the neighborhoods—in the manner of that era. The "big boss" of the place was James H. "Jack" Pollack. Born poor in East Baltimore, he clawed his way up through the worlds of

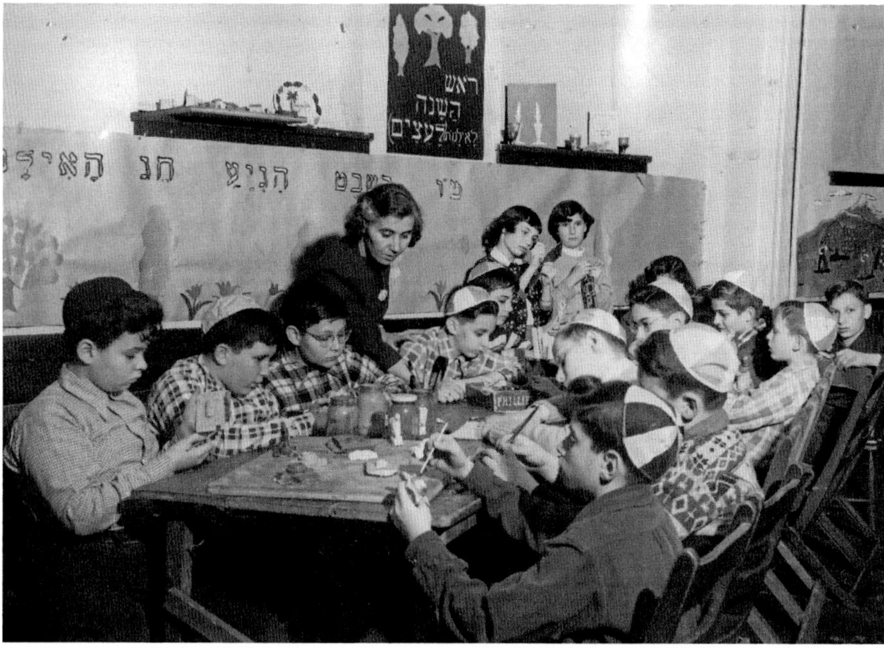

An arts-and-crafts class at Isaac Davidson Hebrew School combines work and play, circa 1948. *Baltimore Hebrew University Archives Collection, 2009.40.5184.*

boxing, bootlegging, insurance and street politics until he was, in Northwest Baltimore at any rate, master of the patronage game. So if you lived in the neighborhood and you needed a job, or to get out of trouble, he would "take care" of the matter—in return for your vote. He is credited with breaking the barrier against the appointment of Jewish judges in Baltimore. Among the beneficiaries: Maurice Cardin, Solomon Liss, Albert Sklar and Paul Dorf.

The department could not in all good conscience leave out the Isaac Davidson Hebrew School on Shirley Avenue, between Park Heights and Reisterstown Road, and it does not. The school was the first to be built as a Hebrew school in Baltimore and, in its curriculum, combined work with play—as the old *cheders* did not. The school grew to be a neighborhood center where young people could meet. There were many clubs, like the Young Judea, and for a time, the building became the uptown branch of the Jewish Educational Alliance (JEA), which brought to the neighborhood even more club activities.

Those of us who grew up in those houses, on those streets, living that life, if we had only known that one day these same houses and neighborhoods were going to be classified as "historic" by the United States Department of the Interior, that historians were going to be studying us and asking questions about the old place, if we had known that it was all going to be an era, we would have paid attention.

Editor's Note: On December 9, 2008, the Lower Park Heights neighborhoods were indeed accepted into and listed officially in the National Register of Historic Places.

Originally published as "Landmark Occasion," August 24, 2007.

The Busiest Streetcar Stop: Old Park Circle

Park Heights Avenue ends up, in its northern extremity, as a country lane winding through leafy, tony Owings Mills. But it begins approximately fourteen miles south, at a point on the map where it branches off of the 3400 block of Reisterstown Road at Druid Park Drive, known to a generation as "Park Circle." The area today is neither park nor circle, but there was a time when it was both, a lost era sometime between the Great Depression, through World War II and into the 1950s.

It was also the busiest streetcar stop between Owings Mills and downtown. Both the No. 5 and No. 33 streetcars ran on that line. Many of them were of the "double" type and, upon taking the sharp turn through the circle, swinging onto Reisterstown Road south and onto Park Heights north, seemed to break apart in the middle. The cars ran north to Belvedere Loop or Manhattan Avenue; south to Pratt and South Streets and Light and Lee, along Reisterstown Road by the Alexander Brown estate, now the site of Mondawmin shopping center, to Fulton Avenue; east to Druid Hill Avenue; and then on a magic carpet to the land of Oz—downtown! Visions of Hutzler's and Hochschild's department stores, the Hippodrome and the Century, Baum's and Awrach and Perl.

Park Circle in the 1940s and 1950s was actually a small park with lawns and benches, full of the era's sights and sounds—in summer, it was a heady mix of balloons and popcorn; in winter, of hot peanuts and teenagers carrying their skates going to and coming from Iceland (Carlin's popular skating rink); and as dusk faded into night, a glow from the oil-can fires the newsboys kept going seemed to light up the night with a faint orange glow.

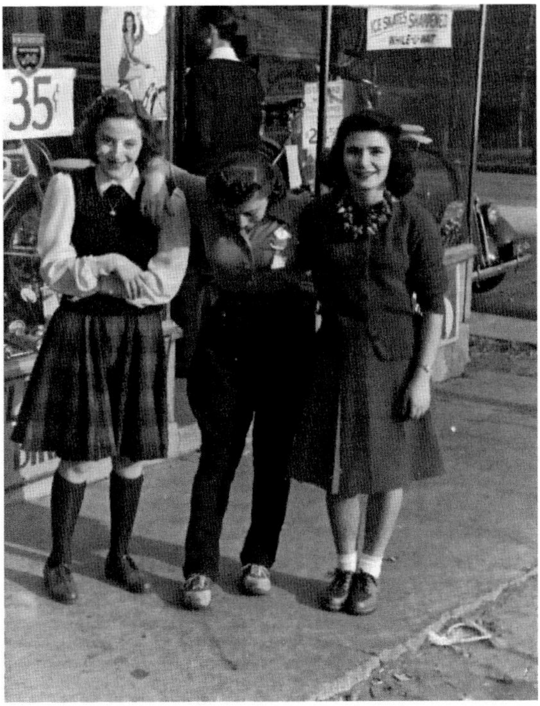

Teenagers Libby Bark, Ida Konig and Eve Topel pal around outside Park Circle's Princeton Cycle Company, circa 1939. *Gift of Stanford C. Reed, 1987.19.37.*

Milling crowds were always going to or coming from the circle's nearby attractions: Druid Hill Park, Carlin's Park, Lapides Deli, Davis's rent-a-bicycle shop, Park Circle Chevrolet, the Hot Shoppe and the White Tower Hamburger Shop. Small wonder Park Circle was one of the busiest streetcar stops in all of Baltimore City.

Carlin's was a park for all seasons. Once you walked through that wondrous and improbable Chinese pagoda that created an entranceway, there was the amusement park, itself a carnival of rides and stellar attractions: the Lindy planes, roller coaster ("Mountain Speedway"), Old Mill (with its Tunnel of Love), Caterpillar, the scooters, the Bug and, of course, the merry-go-round and the sawdust strip of the games of chance, all stacked against the players.

One of the most incredible of Carlin's attractions was the Fun House, a wooden coliseum housing a three-ring circus of rides, shows, acts and nonsense. There was the Hall of Mirrors (one mirror would elongate you, another shrink you, another fatten you), a sliding board three stories high and a revolving turntable on which you tried to cling for dear life while it revolved with increasing speed until it "threw" you off.

For sports enthusiasts, the park offered boxing and wrestling matches in the Green House, which burned down in the 1930s, and ice hockey and general skating sessions in Iceland, which was perhaps Baltimore's first indoor ice-skating rink.

On the same side of the circle were the A&W Hot Shoppe (a favorite of the teenage dating set), famous for its root beer, "cement-thick" milkshakes and carhop service; and the Little Tavern Hamburger shop (which featured a two-inch-square hamburger, smothered in catsup and chopped onions and advertised, "Buy 'em by the bag," which is exactly the way teenagers ate them).

On the other side of the circle was an entrance to Druid Hill Park. Today, the roadway is gone—blocked by a permanent barrier. But in the 1950s, the entrance and the winding roads it led to, through peaceful cathedrals of filtered sunshine and shade, were favorites for bicyclists who converged on the park on Sundays to rent bicycles by the hour from the Princeton Cycle

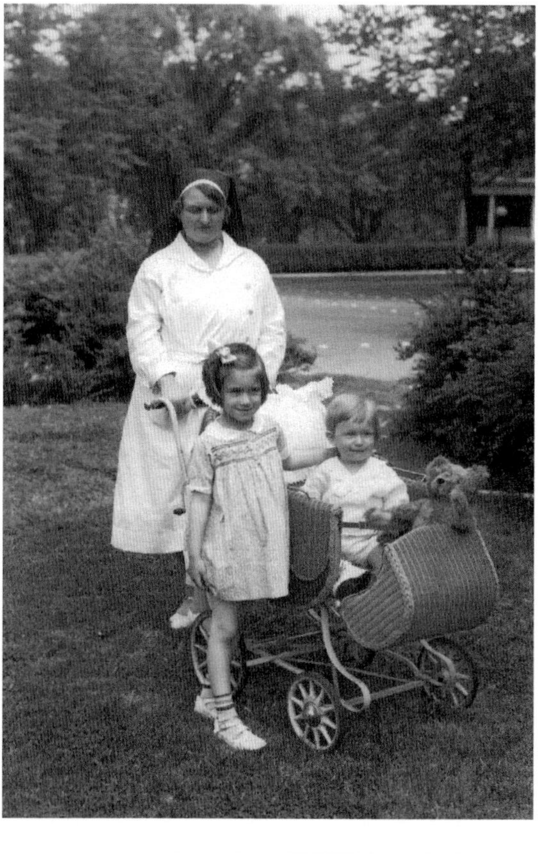

Harry and Amalie Adler, with their nanny, Libby, enjoy the greenery of Druid Hill Park near Park Circle. *Courtesy of Amalie Adler Ascher, 1989.167.9L.*

Shop, at the corner of Reisterstown Road and Druid Park Drive. Samuel and Lucille Davis did a big business renting bicycles, including bicycles built for two. Their son, Bernard "Sonny" Davis, recalls:

> *I started working there when I was eight years old—my father opened at Park Circle in 1936 and left the area in 1951. At our Park Circle shop, we had as many as fifty bikes out at one time—and far more at our location in Druid Hill Park near the reservoir. We charged twenty-five cents an hour, and we were the first in our business to offer bikes with training wheels so kids and moms could keep up with dads.*
>
> *Amazingly, we did a big business after 11:00 p.m., when the waiters and waitresses getting off work at the Hot Shoppe would start their midnight bike-riding in the park.*

Deeper into Druid Hill Park and within walking distance from the streetcar stop in the circle were the Baltimore City municipal swimming pool, the zoo and the tennis courts—which became the playing fields of future Jewish tennis champions, including Eddie Jacobs, Kalman "Buzzy" Hettleman and Adrian Goldberg Hoffman.

Today, if you can make the lights right, you are on a throughway to nowhere. But for a generation that came of age before, during and after World War II, Park Circle in its glory days has become a jewel box, keeping safe the memories of growing up in Jewish Baltimore: the rides of Carlin's Park, the tennis courts of Druid Hill Park, the milkshakes at the Hot Shoppe and the burgers at the Little Tavern. Lighting the reminiscence is the memory of the burnt orange of newsboys' fires flickering in the gray winter twilight.

Originally published as "A Jewel Box," May 27, 2005.

The Corner Drugstores

The corner drugstore is gone, as are the No. 5 and No. 33 streetcars running up and down Park Heights Avenue, the visit to Carlin's Park and the A&W drive-in and the cruises to Tolchester. The white marble-top ice cream tables with their wire legs, the counter stools, the rows of syrup dispensers (which, with their hand-pumping delivery, gave the name "soda jerk" to that genre of counter attendant), the Hendler's, Meadow Gold, Gosman and Suburban Club soda signs—all are today the stuff of pre–World War II nostalgia and the inventory of antique stores.

But for teenagers in Northwest Baltimore, along with the rest of the city from the 1930s through the 1960s, the corner drugstore was a home away from home. Inside, somewhere between the magazine rack and the prescription counter, the teenager (always a male) found the camaraderie that took him through the rite of passage from adolescence into adulthood. They were, individually and collectively, beholden for advice and counsel to the pharmacist, who was sometimes the proprietor but was always known as "Doc," a kindly, authoritative father figure wise in the ways of the world.

Every Jewish neighborhood worthy of its name had a corner drugstore and a Doc. The Doc at Keyworth Pharmacy (Keyworth Avenue at Reisterstown Road) was Joseph "Joe" Wagner, father of Charles "Charlie" Wagner and brother of Emanuel "Mannie" Wagner, who was the Doc at Wagner and Wagner at Reisterstown Road and Gwynns Falls Parkway. Charlie Wagner recalls the era, roughly 1925 to 1965:

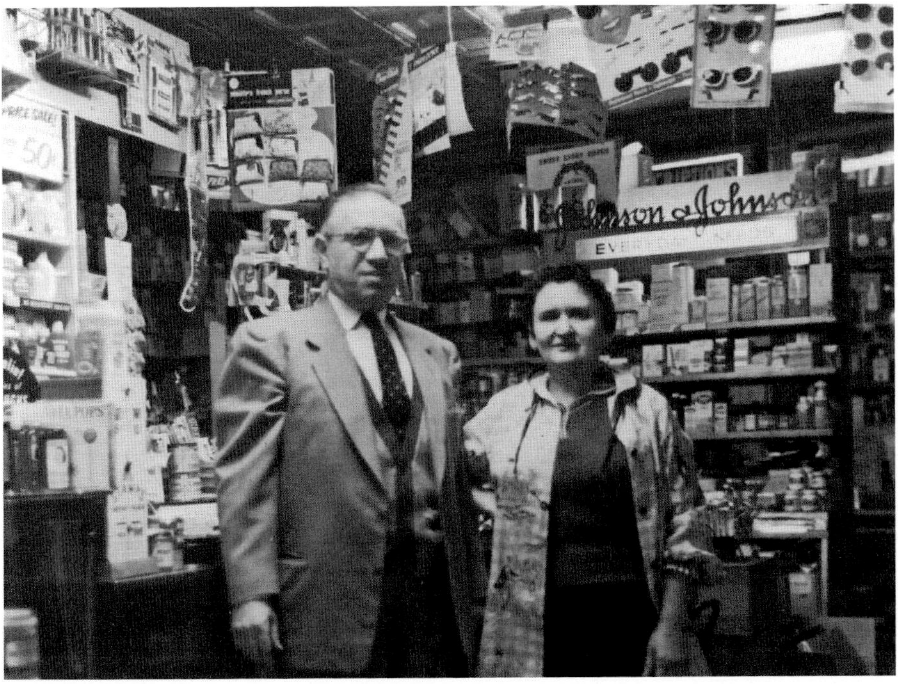

Andrew and Dorothy Silbert stand inside their East Baltimore pharmacy on the corner of Lloyd and Lombard Streets in the late 1950s. *1987.44.2.*

> *The typical Doc worked ninety-nine hours a week. Customers came to him with a cough, and he would give them a bottle of cough syrup. If a customer had something in his eye, Doc would swab it out. A kid would come in with a bleeding knee, Doc would bandage it. In many neighborhoods, the drugstore was the neighborhood clinic and the Doc was the doctor in charge. Most of the Docs took on the job of keeping the kids who hung out there on the straight and narrow.*

The drugstore that holds the record for hanging-out headquarters would appear to be Sachs's. The Doc at Sachs's was Raymond Sachs, and he had to be the most patient of men: "Thirty or forty of us kids from the Shaarei Tfiloh neighborhood would gather at Sachs's on any given Saturday afternoon," Edgar Silver recalled. "Sachs's was our second home."

The Docs offered the most generous of delivery services. Charlie Wagner recalled that from their location at Reisterstown and Gwynns Falls Parkway, Wagner and Wagner delivered to customers as far south as Fulton Avenue, as far east as Auchentoroly Terrace, west to where Douglass High is today and all the way to Liberty Heights and Burleith. Doc Wagner would deliver most anything—a pint of ice cream, a bottle of aspirin, a tube of tooth paste.

Sussman's drugstore was at the corner of Park Heights and Ulman Avenues and was presided over by Doc Hyman Sussman. The store served the contiguous neighborhoods from 1925, when Hyman Sussman opened it, until he closed it in 1964. His daughter, Judy Sussman Culiner, remembers growing up in the place. "Sussman's had a very busy fountain serving milkshakes, chocolate sodas and coddies, and the fountain counter was manned by kids from the neighborhood. My father called the prescription department his 'operating room'—so many kids came in with bruises that he cleaned and dressed. And delivery? He delivered many a chocolate sundae a half mile away!"

Dr. Sidney Sussman was Dr. Hyman Sussman's younger brother, and he worked for Hyman for a while and then became the Doc of SidLen's, his own drugstore at Park Heights and Keyworth Avenues. Judy Sussman Culiner says, "Except for the fact that Uncle Sid's pharmacy was larger than my father's, the formula was the same—a busy fountain selling chocolate sodas and milkshakes, free delivery of just about anything, and a prescription department that was more like today's 'E.R.'"

The Doc at Lewis's Pharmacy on the northwest corner of Park Heights and Rogers Avenues was F. Harold Lewis. His daughter, Barbara Lewis Julius, not only grew up in the store, but also lived over it, along with her parents and her sister. "Yes, we sold sodas, in particular lemon phosphates, and snowballs. My father didn't sell coddies but he kept a container of long, thin pretzels and oatmeal cookies on the counter. We were not far from Arlington elementary, and in those days, every lunch time, a lot of the kids would come into Lewis's with their lunch and buy a soda to go with it. My father carried a whistle in his pocket. When the kids got too noisy, he would give out a shrill blast or two to quiet them down."

Zentz's Pharmacy, according to Gerry Zentz, was, from his observation, probably the largest and the busiest of the some twenty corner drugstores from Rogers Avenue to Park Circle that flourished from the 1930s through the 1960s.

> *My father, Doc Milton Zentz, had an uncommon touch for the business. Probably most of the people living on Narcissus, Jonquil, Nelson and Gist Avenues were Zentz customers. We kept two trucks busy delivering the year around, and during the flu season, we added two more. Doc Zentz knew each and every one of his customers, so well in fact that sometimes he conducted business with them in Yiddish.*

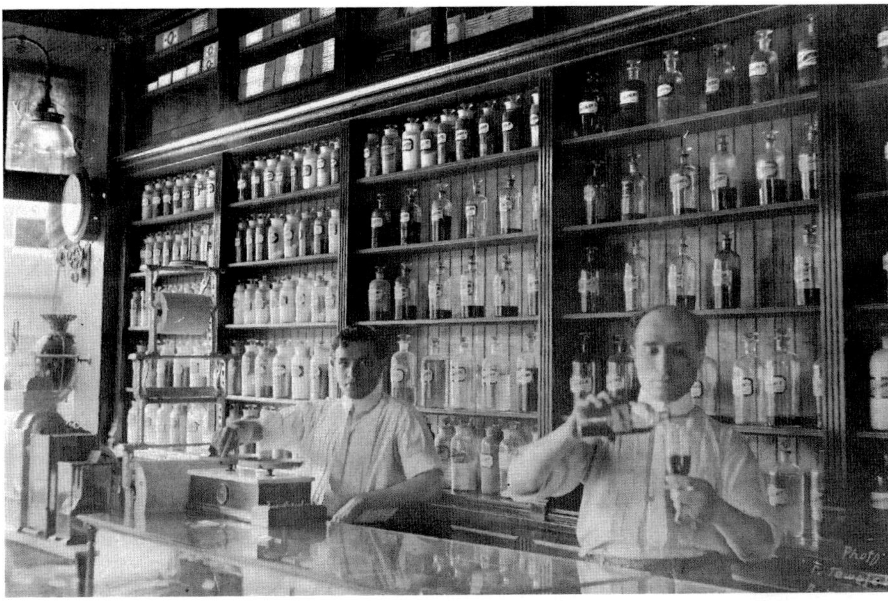

Pharmacist Abraham Hillman heralded the migration of Baltimore Jews to Northwest Baltimore, moving his pharmacy to lower Park Heights in 1922. Abraham and an assistant stand behind the counter of the Eden Street Pharmacy, shown here in its original location at Lexington and Eden Streets in 1904. *Gift of Hilda Hillman, 2008.24.1.*

But there were many other corner drugstores, and many other Docs, serving the Jewish neighborhoods. To name some, but surely not all: Abramowitz's at 4300 Park Heights Avenue; Avalon Pharmacy, 4952 Park Heights Avenue; Beeli's, 5133 Park Heights Avenue, Brill's, 5500 Park Heights Avenue; Brookhill, 6715 Reisterstown Road; Diener's, 4817 Pimlico Road; Hillman's, Park Heights at Cottage Avenue; Kling's, 4685 Park Heights Avenue; Lachman's, 5024 Park Heights Avenue; Manheimer's at 2502 Eutaw Place; Rudies's, 3102 West North Avenue; Schapiro's, 4601 Park Heights Avenue: Shure's, 5024 Park Heights Avenue and 3801 Liberty Road; Triangle, 3845 Park Heights Avenue; Suburban, Reisterstown Road at Slade Avenue; Weiner's, 5501 Reisterstown Road; and Mt. Washington Pharmacy, Smith and Kelly Avenues.

Today's huge conglomerate-style drug chains that have replaced corner drugstores do offer, it has to be said, more items to choose from (the corner drugstores did not sell outdoor grills) and, arguably, lower prices. And it takes nothing away from the conscientious and overworked pharmacists who serve at the prescription counters of these monster chains to say that they are indeed doctors of pharmacy. But you are hard pressed to find one who is a "Doc."

Originally published as "Prescription for Success," November 30, 2001.

Riding the Crest: Hilltop Shopping Center

Over the years, Northwest Baltimore has enjoyed a number of neighborhood centers that were popular with the Jewish community (Park Heights and Belvedere, Liberty Road and Old Court). Among those fondly remembered is the Hilltop Shopping Center, the complex of stores, restaurants and the movie house crowding the southeast corner of Reisterstown Road and Rogers Avenue.

From 1956 well into the 1980s, this busy complex offered visitors the well-known Baltimore family stores, the Crest movie theater and Mandell-Ballow's delicatessen. The Rogers Avenue Synagogue, a block or so to the east, served its congregants in the neighborhood, including many who had moved to the Rogers Avenue community from West Baltimore. Just above Rogers, on the east side of Reisterstown Road, were Weiner's Pharmacy, the B&B Food Market and Greenfeld Brothers Hardware. And across Reisterstown Road was Barry Levinson's legendary diner. Together, for almost forty years, the area was a destination for a generation that would project it into the mythology of Northwest Baltimore.

The Crest opened on February 26, 1949, with *Adventures of Don Juan,* starring Errol Flynn and Viveca Lindfors. In those days, ticket prices were twenty-five cents at Monday through Friday matinees and forty cents in the evening and all day Saturday, Sunday and holidays. Children were admitted for eighteen cents—all shows. A full-page ad in the *Evening Sun* on February 25 announced the Crest's grand opening the next day at noon and presented the theater as state of the art: "Seventeen hundred seats, air-conditioned, twin-smoking loges."

Mandell-Ballow's was a Jewish deli in the "overwhelm 'em" style of both Mandell's of Baltimore Street and Ballow's of West North Avenue, offering monstrous sandwiches of dizzying complexity and desserts of mountainous proportions. The restaurant accommodated three hundred at a time and, in certain of its years, was open twenty-four hours, so it became a headquarters of sorts for politicians choosing their candidates, for businessmen striking their deals and for race-track types touting their favorites. There was a banquet hall downstairs, the Fiesta Room, which was the scene of many a bar and bat mitzvah party.

Jay Mandell, son of proprietor Joe Mandell, worked at Mandell-Ballow's after he graduated college, beginning in 1963. "We were doing business in a time before the fast food chains opened, and so we were really *the* place to eat in Northwest Baltimore," he says. "When the show broke at the Crest, hundreds of people flooded our doors. They formed a line all the way back to the Crest. We had a soda fountain with stools and our own bakery. Our big seller was our Number 179 sandwich—corned beef, cole slaw and Russian dressing."

Recalls his sister, Barbara Mandell Desser: "I was in high school in 1958 and worked after school and weekends in the deli, wherever they needed me. At the register, in the bake shop, at the soda fountain. I helped make sundaes. Do you know that we had green, pink, blue and yellow whipped cream? Everything served at Mandell-Ballow was special. We pickled our own corned beef. Nothing you buy in a deli today compares with the quality we served." Also in the center were the Saler's Dairy, Sheer and Dreibon

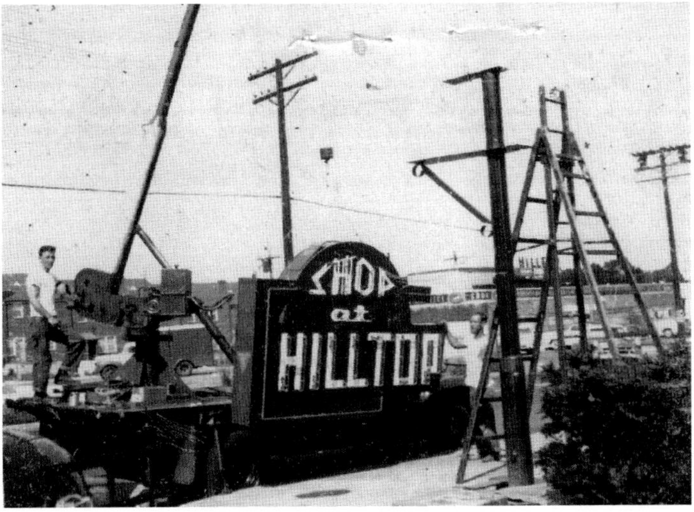

This "Shop at Hilltop" sign was created and installed by the Triangle Sign Company, a Jewish-owned business formed in 1931. *Gift of Louis G. Hecht, 1998.16.82.*

kosher butchers, Eddie's supermarket, Barcelona Nut and Candy, the Hilltop Bowling Alley and Holzman's Bakery.

Holzman's was one of the most popular of the Jewish-owned retail bakeries in Baltimore. At one time, according to Willie Holzman, there were as many as six Holzman's bakeries in operation throughout the area. Remembers Mr. Holzman: "We opened in 1948 and we were there until 1979—thirty-one years. Hilltop in those days was a very busy shopping center, and ours was a busy store. It took twelve people to keep it going."

Across Reisterstown Road from Hilltop was the Diner, gone these many years and later occupied by Hilltop Liquors. The Diner, according to Irving Lansman, whose A&L kosher-food distribution company was a supplier to the Diner, "was founded right after the war by Mike Siegel, who sold it to the Stamas brothers. The menu was very Jewish—they featured bagels and lox, blintzes, matzoh ball soup and, at their counter, halvah." As it has been so lovingly portrayed in Barry Levinson's movie of the same name, the Diner was more than a restaurant; it was a hangout for a group of neighborhood young men in a rite of passage through their teens, using wit and verbal sparring to ease the way.

On the High Holidays, Rogers Avenue at Reistertown Road was a scene of milling crowds coming and going to the nearby Rogers Avenue Synagogue. The shul had its roots deep in the West Baltimore of the early 1900s and, in 1929, was known as the Ohr Knesseth Israel congregation. In 1950, the Anshe Sphard congregation of 4 North Broadway and the Ohr Knesseth Israel Congregation of West Franklin Street merged to form the Ohr Knesseth Israel-Anshe Sphard, known, beginning in 1951, as the Rogers Avenue Synagogue.

In the late 1970s and early 1980s, the Reisterstown and Rogers area was caught up in harsh socioeconomic changes. In time, the movie house, the Diner, the synagogue, Weiner's Pharmacy, B&B Food Market, Greenfeld's and many of the stores in the center either closed or left the area and opened elsewhere. The center, built by the Myerberg Brothers and designed by architect Julius Myerberg, was sold to Steven Sibel.

The buildings that housed the familiar and wildly popular Jewish institutions are still there and recognizable, too. But for Jews who have vivid memories of Mandell-Ballow, the Crest, Weiner's, the Rogers Avenue Synagogue and the rest, these buildings are monuments to another time.

Originally published as "Riding the Crest," June 25, 1999.

Different as Children, Different as Adults

On the Sunday afternoon of March 23, 2003, about thirty people gathered in the home of Barry and Janice Salzman in Stevenson for a reunion. Most had in common a quirky uniqueness: all were Jewish and lived in Baltimore but did not grow up in Jewish Baltimore. They were born and raised and lived their lives as Jews in—of all unlikely places—Brooklyn, Maryland, and Glen Burnie and North Anne Arundel County. Their distance from the mainstream of Baltimore Jewry defined them as children and bonded them as adults.

"Growing up in those neighborhoods," Janice Greenberg Salzman says, "we knew that we were different." By "neighborhood," she means Brooklyn, a historically non-Jewish neighborhood in deep South Baltimore, then made up mostly of steelworkers. She goes on to say:

> *Of course you felt it most at Christmastime and the Jewish High Holidays. We didn't celebrate Christmas, and they didn't celebrate Jewish holidays. We lived out of sync with our neighbors.*
>
> *I experienced one particularly telling incident. When I was in junior high, PS 239, student members of Future Teachers of America were sometimes asked to take over a class of younger children while the teacher, for whatever reason, had to be out of the class. I was asked to take over the opening exercises for a first-grade class. I led them through the Pledge of Allegiance and the Twenty-third Psalm—and then, to my surprise—I was leading them through the hymn, "Yes, Jesus Loves Me." That's what it was like, growing up Jewish in Brooklyn in the 1950s.*

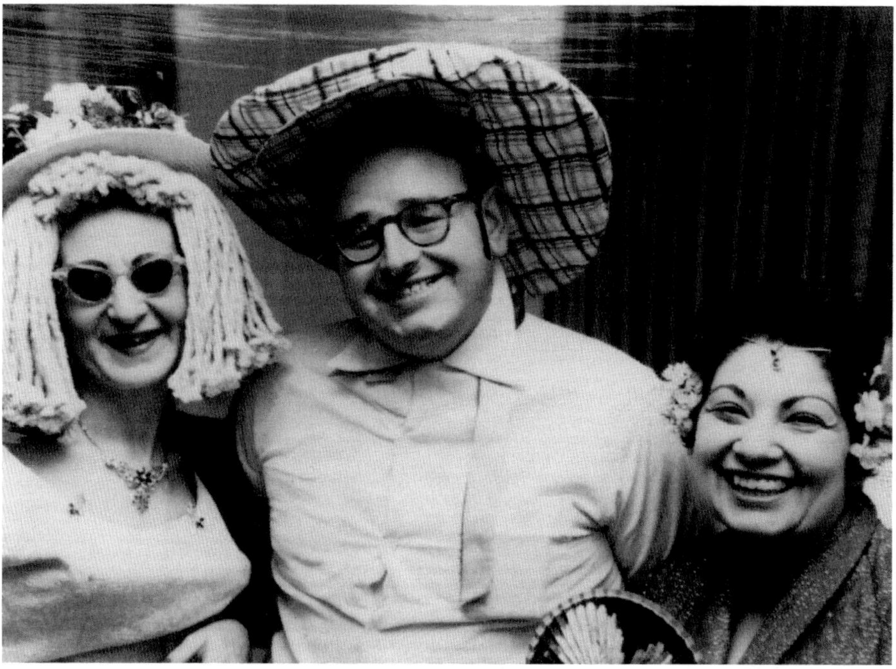

A small population didn't stop these Brooklyn, Maryland families from celebrating their Jewish identities. Here, Har-Brook Hebrew Congregation founding members Evelyn Markowitz, Milton Markowitz and Gertrude Greenberg are all dressed up for Purim festivities, circa 1955. *Gift of Mrs. Markowitz and Mrs. Greenberg, 1993.29.14.*

Others at the reunion included Myra Lowenthal; Lenny, Philip and Ricky Schimburg; Gerald and Daniel Leibowitz; Lynn and Ted Weisberg; and David Greenberg. Abe Teitler was not there, but his presence must surely have been felt. In 1945, he had come to Baltimore from New York with his wife to work for the U.S. government—as did thousands of others in those World War II days. His first problem—where to live? Coming from a strong Jewish background, he looked for housing in a Jewish neighborhood, where he thought he and his wife would be comfortable. But because Baltimore was caught in a severe housing shortage, the Teitlers, to their discomfort, found housing (and lucky, at that!) in—of all places—Harundale. It was a community of ticky-tacky houses, just below Glen Burnie in Anne Arundel County, thrown together overnight, lived in fitfully by shipyard workers sleeping between shifts at Bethlehem Shipyards. Not your father's Jewish neighborhood.

But they made do, adapted and waited for things to change. Things did, beginning with a knock on their door on a Sunday afternoon in September 1949. "The caller was a Mrs. Robinson," Abe Teitler recalled. "She said that

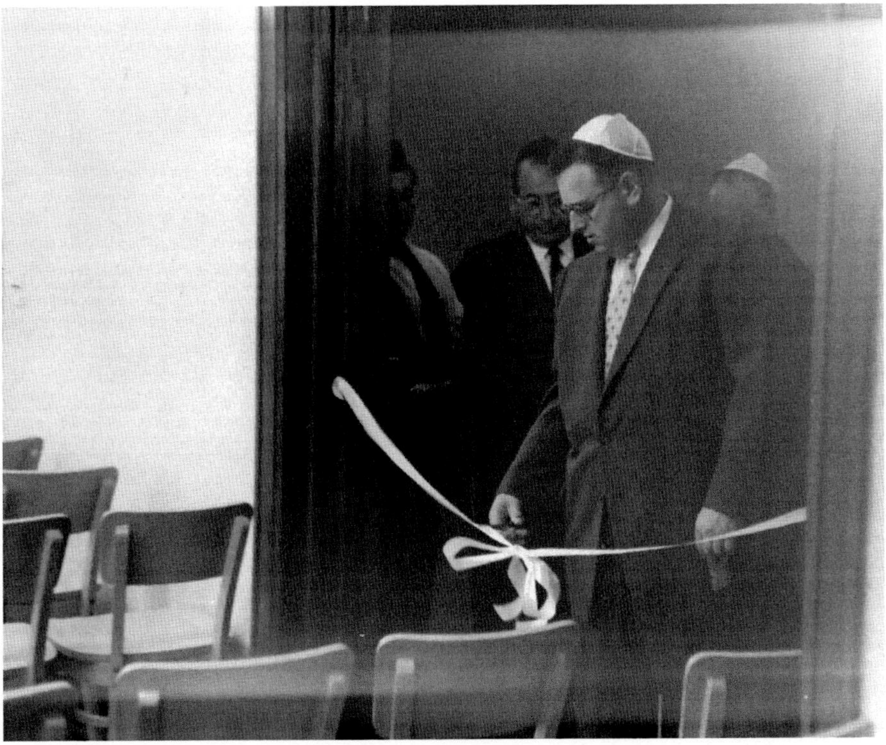

Rabbi Israel Goldman looks on as Milton Markowitz wields shears to cut the ribbon at the new Har-Brook Hebrew Congregation synagogue, September 1955. *Gift of Mrs. Markowitz and Mrs. Greenberg, 1993.29.1.*

she understood we were a Jewish family and that she, too, was Jewish, living in Harundale and raising children. She said she wanted to provide a Jewish education for her children and would we, too, be interested in forming a Sunday school." That conversation led to the creation of a school held in the Teitler house. "We approached Dr. Louis Kaplan, then head of Jewish education in Baltimore, and he provided excellent advice and helped us to set up the school."

The school eventually folded into the school of the newly forming Har-Brook Hebrew Congregation in September 1952—its first services, led by Rabbi Robert Chernoff, were held above the firehouse on Ritchie Highway. Founding members included the families of Milton and Evelyn Markowitz, Melvin and Gertie Greenberg, Melvin Hoffman, Howard Mishkin, Cecelia and Philip Salsbury and Howard Rosen. In 1955, the congregation was able to buy and remodel an old frame house at 4303 Ritchie Highway and convert it into a synagogue and school.

David Greenberg, Janice's brother, was at the reunion, too:

> *I remember as a kid we would go to High Holiday services at the firehouse on Ritchie Highway. We had about fifty families and used the Conservative Siddur. Many Jewish families were living down there because the family business was located there. In our case, my father had a jewelry store. We all went to the neighborhood elementary and junior high schools, but for high school, I went to City—more than an hour's ride on the No. 6 bus—and my sister went to Western; she, too, had a very long ride.*

Evelyn Radesky Markowitz was also at the reunion:

> *At age eighty-six, I'm the bubbe of this whole gang. My family moved to Brooklyn in 1929, along with many other Jewish families that opened small businesses in the neighborhood. My father's men's furnishings store was at 400 Patapsco Avenue, and we lived behind and over the store. Like the other Jewish kids, I went to elementary school at PS 203 on Fourth Street and, for junior high and high school, to Southern High. I not only grew up in Brooklyn, I met my future husband there, and, except for the past few years, I lived there all my life.*
>
> *You have to remember that all over Curtis Bay, Fairfield, Glen Burnie, and Harundale, were Jews operating small businesses who were drawn to worship together. They went first to Anshe Amunah in South Baltimore and then, in 1952, when that congregation moved uptown, we formed the Har-Brook Synagogue.*

Are the Jews who grew up in Brooklyn, Glen Burnie and Anne Arundel County "different" as adults? Janice Greenberg Salzman says, "Yes. I think we have a healthier understanding of the non-Jewish world. That knowledge has made us better Jews." Evelyn Markowitz agrees:

> *We never experienced anti-Semitism—ever. On Chanukah we invited all the gentile kids into our homes, and on Christmas they invited us. Has growing up Jewish in this non-Jewish world made us different? Absolutely. I think we were better educated as citizens and human beings than we would have been had we grown up confined to a life lived along Park Heights. Ours was a more worldly, a more interesting, life than our friends' in the Northwest ghetto. We were different as Jewish children, and we are different as Jewish adults.*

Originally published as "The Brooklyn Bridge," March 25, 2005.

PART 2

Crises and Causes

Generation after generation, Jewish Baltimoreans have participated fully in the wonders of America. Here they have thrived, finding opportunity to advance for themselves and for their children. But like other Americans, Baltimore Jews have been subject to the great crises of their time—epidemic, depression and war. They have also been participants in many causes—ensuring the welfare of other Jews, here and abroad, pressing for full participation in public life and joining in movements like women's suffrage and civil rights.

In these four stories, we encounter Jewish Baltimoreans enmeshed in memorable crises and causes. In some, they—like other city residents—are victims of circumstance; in others, they are actively engaged, seeking to make a difference. For many today, the events described here are, at best, dimly recalled. But for others, these historical scenes remain vivid and profoundly moving.

The Deadly Winter

On the cold morning of Sunday, January 19, 1919, ten men dressed in black were gathered around the door of 1420 East Fayette Street in East Baltimore. They were pallbearers, and together they lifted a casket to shoulder height. Eight more men, younger than the pallbearers, formed in front of the casket, two by two. These younger men made up a choir; singing, swaying, they started the procession, to the dirge we know as "*El Malei Rachamim*," and with a slow, heavy walk they led the procession west along Fayette Street.

Crowds lined the curbs and, with unhidden tears, showed their grief. Twenty minutes later, the procession arrived at the Aitz Chayim synagogue at 15 South Eden Street near Baltimore Street. They had come to bury Ben Dorman.

The size of the standing-room-only crowd inside the synagogue suggested the reputation and community presence of Mr. Dorman. Rabbi Reuben Rifkin reminded the congregants of Dorman's meaningful and productive life in Jewish Baltimore: founder of Aitz Chayim synagogue and the Benjamin Dorman Lodge of the Brith Abraham and active in Adath Bnai Israel. He spoke of how life, as it must after grievous loss, moves on.

Still, this death held an extra dimension of sadness; Benjamin Dorman was a tragic statistic in the historic flu epidemic of 1918. "No disease the world has ever known," writes John M. Barry in his *The Great Influenza*, "even remotely resembles the great influenza epidemic of 1918." Twenty million, some say fifty million, died in cities, farms and, particularly, army camps around the world. Here in Baltimore, too, the devastation in its horror was Biblical. In the approximately 120 days of the epidemic (October 1918 through January 1919), about four thousand Baltimoreans died.

No exact figures exist for how many of those Baltimoreans were Jewish, but interpolating, that number is probably about four hundred—mostly the very young and the very old. Mr. Dorman was sixty-eight, old in those years—and he was not the only Jew in Baltimore to be buried that day. There were so many that the funeral parlors could not keep up. Sons dug graves for fathers (and mothers); fathers, for sons (and daughters). Streetcar riders wore masks. Fines were levied against men smoking on the cars (it was thought that smoke carried flu germs.) Car tokens were bathed daily in an antiseptic solution.

At certain times during the worst of the epidemic, all public places in Baltimore were closed—department stores, libraries, restaurants, the schools, all of the churches and synagogues. Classes were suspended at Johns Hopkins University.

"Everyone was out sick," said Jim Duffy, writing in 2002 of the flu epidemic of 1918 in Baltimore for *Johns Hopkins Public Health*, the magazine

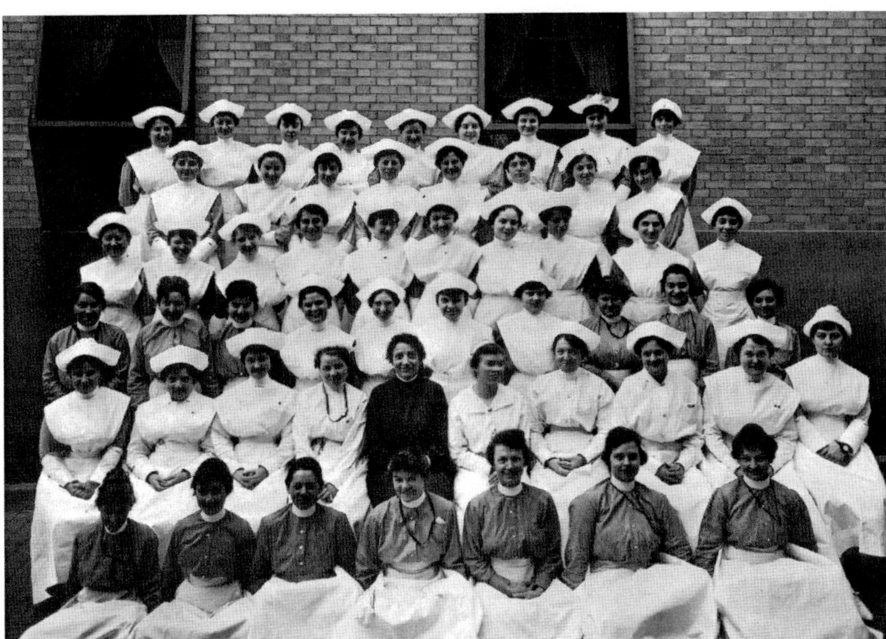

This 1918 class of Sinai Hospital nurses finished their training just as the influenza epidemic was born. The next two years would test their skills to the limit. *1988.115.3.*

of the Bloomberg School of Public Health. "There were too few milkmen, too few firefighters, too few telephone operators. The city didn't have enough workers to process death certificates. Hospitals were overwhelmed. At Hopkins, flu patients occupied six wards and then the hospital closed its doors—it simply could not handle any more patients. Three staff physicians, three medical students and six nurses died in the epidemic."

Sinai Hospital, known in 1918 as the Hebrew Hospital, recorded, according to Paul Umansky, a retired Sinai employee, that "by October 6, it was impossible to get anyone into our hospital. We could not even give advice, we sent people directly to the Health Department. Our hospital was full, and taxed to the limit."

Among the many in Baltimore's Jewish families to die in the flu epidemic of 1918 was Rebecca Katzen, grandmother of Karen Pine. Ms. Pine recalls the oral history in the family: "My mother remembers that the doctor told my grandfather to 'Open all the windows and let in the cold air.' Which we

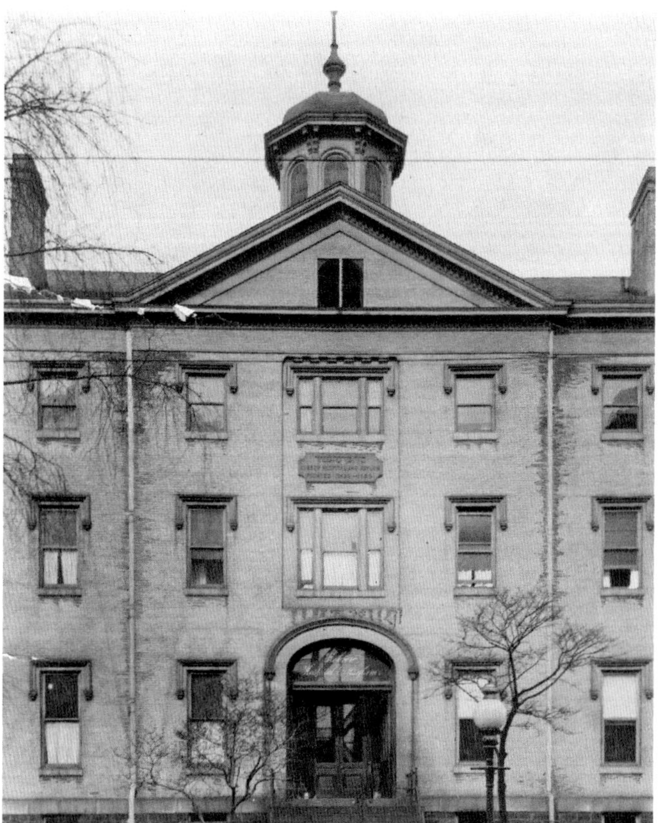

Erected in 1868, the Hebrew Hospital and Asylum on East Monument Street was one of the many Baltimore hospitals overwhelmed by the influenza epidemic of 1918. *Gift of Earl Pruce, 1985.90.11.*

have all felt ever since was the wrong advice. And one of my aunts was a triplet and two of those triplets died of the flu."

Elmer Klavans's aunt, Sophie Shapiro, died at age twenty-five, and his cousin, Bernard Schreiber, died at five. Sheila Eller's great aunt, Rebecca Simonoff, died at age thirteen. Ms. Eller recalls, "They diagnosed her with flu on a Tuesday and buried her Thursday, forty-eight hours later." Samuel Shulman recalls, "My uncle, Morris Bronner, died in the flu epidemic. We lived in Highlandtown. I remember caskets piled up on the sidewalk of the funeral home across the street. My mother made us wear a camphor pack around our neck."

From the view atop its highest hill, the tombstones of the United Hebrew Cemetery, on Washington Boulevard, south and west of Baltimore City, stand as battalions of sentries—gray, silent and somber. If you walk among these tombstones, you will see, almost hidden, tiny gravestones not much larger than a child's schoolbook. These are the fading remembrances of some of the Jewish children who died in Baltimore in the flu epidemic of 1918. Time and weather have softened the outlines of those names. Engraved so clearly eighty years ago, today the stones only whisper the names.

All of the tombstones read "1918": David Cohen, age seven; Abraham Feldman, sixteen; Aleck Tucker, fourteen; Israel Rosenberg, nineteen; Bertha Goldberg, sixteen; Ella Block, eighteen; Dora Fleisher, thirty-one; Michael Maggid, thirty-eight; Ida Eskalov, nineteen; Lillian Levy, seventeen; three children of the Berkow family, side by side—Ida, Joseph and a third name that is indecipherable. Leroy Smith, caretaker of the cemetery with extensive knowledge of it, says, "Families brought in two and sometimes three children all together. They buried them side by side, which explains the Berkow graves."

And Helen Miriam Sandler, age four, sister of the author.

Following the ceremonies at Aitz Chaim, the casket was transported by hearse to the Adath Bnai Israel at 114 Aisquith Street. Here, the rabbi preached a second sermon. Then the mourners filed out onto Aisquith Street, the casket was returned to the hearse and the funeral procession moved on to the Aitz Chaim Cemetery, near Lansdowne.

And when, in that long-ago January, the flu disappeared, humanity, according to historian Gina Kolata, "had been struck by a disease that killed more people in a few months' time than any other illness in the history of the world."

But the world, the country and the city proved resilient. As did Jewish Baltimore. Synagogue life resumed with vigor; the Jewish Educational

Alliance was back to offering a full slate of programming; families celebrated births, b'nai mitzvah and anniversaries; the charities were energized as they had not been before. Reports of lavish wedding parties reappeared in the newly created *Baltimore Jewish Times*.

Rabbi Rifkin, preaching at the funeral of Benjamin Dorman in January 1919, had it right. Jewish life did go on, albeit with a keener sense of its fragility.

Originally published as "Epidemic Proportions," April 22, 2005.

Hard Times, Shattered Dreams

Generations accustomed to runaway wealth can find it hard to believe what their parents, grandparents and great-grandparents went through during the Great Depression of the 1930s. Times were so hard for them that one out of four could not find a job; family businesses were going bankrupt by the dozens; some Jewish families simply did not have enough money to buy food or pay rent, much less enjoy such amenities as the automobile or telephone (though everybody seems to have had a radio). They went to bed at night taking comfort in the knowledge that they still had money in the bank, only to wake up in the morning to discover that they did not. Their life's savings had been wiped out.

Some men were known to leave the house in the morning and spend all day walking the streets looking for work. They would come home, have dinner and, in the morning, start the routine all over again, in too many cases without success. Some left town to find work elsewhere. Some, rather than face the pain of debt, or seeing their family starving, committed suicide.

The Depression affected Baltimore's Jews as individuals and families in different ways. Some were affected profoundly, others somewhat and still others not at all. Alvin Katzenstein was in his late teens when the stock market crashed, bringing the 1920s, with all of its excesses, to a dismal end. He recalls:

> *My father and uncles were in the clothing business and doing well when the bad times came. The customers had no money to buy at the stores, and*

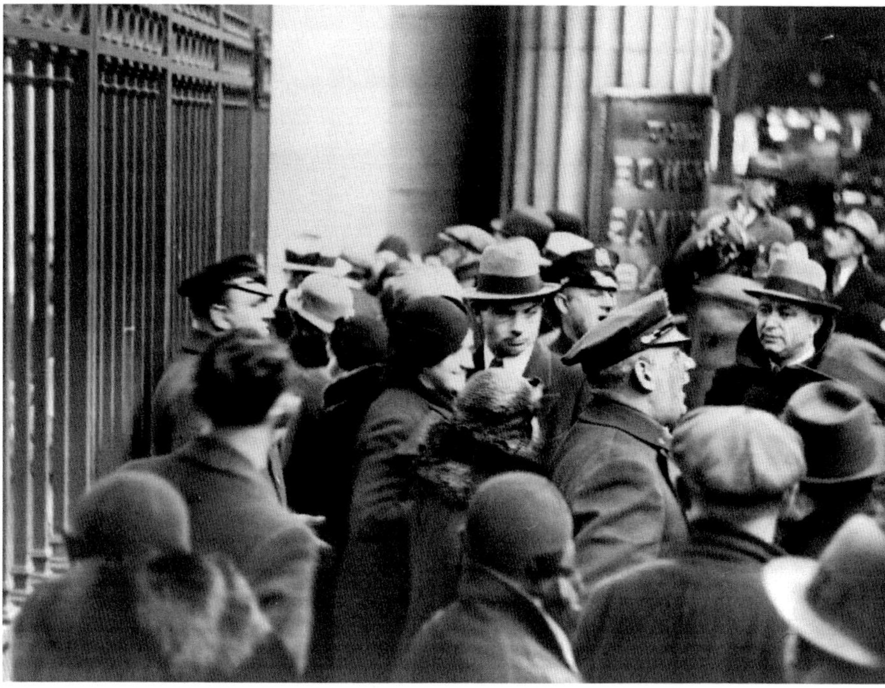

The Great Depression saw banks fail across America, leaving no city untouched. Here, policemen turn customers away, announcing that a bank has closed. *Courtesy of the Library of Congress, CP 2.2012.3.*

> *so the stores stopped ordering. It wasn't long before my father was out of business, and several uncles struggled to stay in business. It seemed to me that everybody was out of work, and everywhere downtown you could see long lines of men applying for jobs that weren't there.*
>
> *Very often, to save money, two and three families would sell two of the houses they owned and all move into the third. That's about what happened to us. The side of the family that lived on North Avenue sold their home and moved in with us on Linden Avenue. I was a sophomore at Johns Hopkins, but I had to drop out. My family simply couldn't meet the tuition payments. Our temple seats, too, became a victim of the Depression. And I remember one Rosh Hashanah, though we could no longer afford tickets, my father suggested we go over to Baltimore Hebrew at Madison Avenue and see if they would let us in anyway.*

Alvin's wife, Dorothy Tucker Katzenstein, has her own memories of growing up in the Great Depression:

We lived around North Avenue and Presbury Street and to pick up a few dollars a week we took in roomers. My father, Jacob, who had been a farmer in Argentina, and was a Hebrew scholar quite capable of teaching Jewish studies at any level, could find no students—and no other kind of work, either. So this gentle and educated man got himself a pushcart and every Wednesday and Friday morning he somehow managed to stock it with fresh fish, and he would push his cart through the alleys of West Baltimore, selling fish. He did that to support six people.

Walter Sondheim recalls:

I was twenty-two years old and working in the executive training program at Hochschild, Kohn. Business was terrible. Salaries were being cut, people were being laid off. I recall clearly the day the banks closed. It was Monday, March 4, 1933. Hochschild's had a policy of cashing paychecks for teachers. Well, that Friday, in came all of these teachers' checks, the banks were closed and we did not have the cash on hand to cover the checks. We notified City Hall right away, and miraculously, they said they had the cash to cover the checks, but we would have to go over right away. I rode in a Brink's truck to City Hall, holding a bag of teachers' checks and, coming back, sacks of cash. What a week that was! People were frantic; there was no money to buy anything. Nobody could be paid. Everybody's checking and savings account was frozen in the closed banks. To live, you had only the money in your pocket or under the mattress.

Among those who did not feel the sting of the Depression at all was the group of German Jews who gathered at the Belvedere Hotel—men tuxedoed, women bejeweled—stepping from chauffeur-driven limousines into the bright lights on the evening of November 29, 1929, a full month after the crash. This was the seventieth annual Harmony Circle Ball, the "coming-out" party to introduce the Jewish debutantes to German Jewish society. If any of the Jews in the assemblage of that sparkling evening was suffering from the joblessness or the stock market crash, you could not tell it from this evening's pageantry—the crowd, the extravagant setting of the ballroom, had an ambiance, it was reported, "reminiscent of the parties in the novels of F. Scott Fitzgerald." What depression?

Dr. Sylvan Shane lived in the 3100 block of Reisterstown Road:

There were five children and my parents—seven of us. My father managed to keep us all well fed from the modest living he made from his shoe store. I

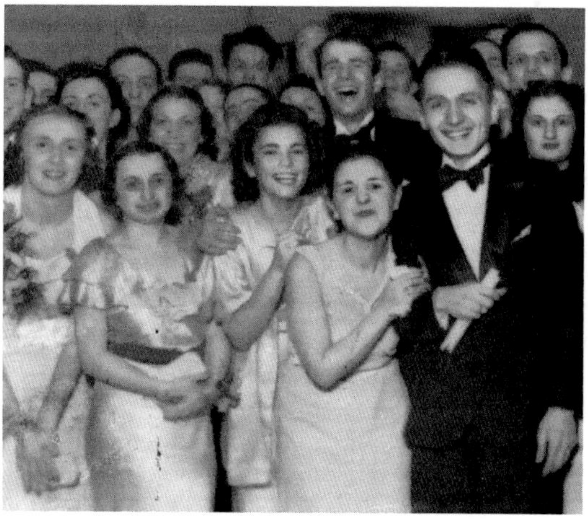

Not even the Great Depression could repress the tenth anniversary of the Beth Tfiloh Annual Cotillion. *Gift of Ann Sue Grossman, 1999.20.9.*

> *do remember, though, that once we had our telephone disconnected because we couldn't pay the bill. I saw plenty of poverty on the block. A few doors down there was a family—mother, father, thirteen kids. They just didn't have enough food to go around. All the kids worked. They sold popcorn and balloons in Druid Hill Park, newspapers at Carlin's Park. But my mother and some other neighbors took food down to them, often. I left Baltimore in 1936 because my father did not have enough money to pay the tuition for me to go to Johns Hopkins—three hundred dollars.*

Jastrow Levin remembers life in the Depression:

> *With help from friends, I was able to graduate Beloit College in 1933 with a major in biological sciences. I looked for a job with a university or a hospital or city or state health department. There were simply no jobs to be had. So I looked for a job teaching, and I couldn't find a job there either. Finally, I got a position teaching in an Annapolis high school. But I was no sooner there then they cut my salary. So I moved on to teach at City College, and they cut my salary, even further. Well, things were so bad that we converted our house at 2104 Chelsea Terrace into three apartments for my brother and his wife, my sister and her husband, and my wife and me. We didn't have enough money to live on, but we lived on it.*

Willard Hackerman was thirteen in 1931 and in the eighth grade at Forest Park, then a junior high as well as high school. He recalls:

The cafeteria lunch that they sold featured lettuce sandwiches, for a nickel. Just lettuce, between two slices of bread. A little mayonnaise. I graduated from Poly in 1935, and that year they played two Poly-City games. Admission to the second game was a can of food, to be given to the poor.

There was no money around for scholarships, so to matriculate at Hopkins, I asked if they would accept my tuition on the "installment plan." They had never heard of such an arrangement, but they agreed. My parents paid part of the $45 a month. I supplemented the tuition by working for several of my professors—forty cents an hour, forty hours a week—on top of my schooling schedule. I saw unemployed men selling apples at Howard and Lexington Streets and men lined up for loaves of bread in the neighborhoods. After I had graduated, there were no jobs in engineering, and even if there were, Jewish boys would never have gotten them. I knew engineering graduates who sold shoes for the duration of the Depression.

Daniel Goldman, whose family owned and operated Paramount Clothing Company in the 1930s in the loft district made up almost entirely of Jewish merchants and manufacturers, saw it all and remembers: "It was awful. Business was terrible. The banks weren't lending money and what you could get manufactured you had to sell at give-away prices. It was impossible to make a profit. The big manufacturers—Greif and Schoeneman—survived, but many of the smaller ones went bankrupt."

In 1934, Harry Greenstein, executive director of the Associated Jewish Charities, summed up the crisis for the Jewish community in a speech delivered to his board:

After three years of mass unemployment, it should not be difficult to visualize the physical suffering of these Jewish men, women and children, their emotional distress, and their spiritual agony. These men and women are losing their morale, their self-confidence, their self-respect. They are not the usual charity cases. They are people who have been caught in this economic whirlpool, sucked down through no fault of their own, unable to keep their heads above water. They need help. And we are providing it, preventing the evictions of families from their homes because of nonpayment of rent, and providing food where there is no food.

"No Jewish family in Baltimore," he emphasized, "has as yet been denied relief. Not one deserving Jew requiring medical or hospital care has been denied help."And a year later, Associated president Walter Sondheim told his board, trying to stem the flood of opinion arguing for suspension of Associated support for cultural activities, that "we must think in terms of the comforts of life that make a difference between bare existence and simply living. Our clients are human beings."

But life went on and, some of it, considering the times, with surprising normality. Reading the society pages during those years, Miss Elizabeth Roten, who spent the summer in Europe, returned to her home on Eutaw Place. Dr. and Mrs. Erwin Mayer, with their children, Jane and Erwin Jr., returned from Wabanaki Lodge in Maine. Mr. and Mrs. Joseph Berman and Mr. and Mrs. Charles Cohen returned from the Catskills.

Mr. and Mrs. Israel Friedman of 2311 Anoka Avenue announced the marriage of their daughter Sadye to Mr. Ray Goldberg. The couple planned to honeymoon in New York. Mr. and Mrs. Isaac Friedman of 2704 Oswego Avenue announced the marriage of their daughter, Annette, to Mr. Harry Gerson. The marriage took place in the New Howard Hotel. The Suburban Club announced that "entertained at the Club recently" were Mrs. Sidney Westheimer, Mrs. Louis Baer, Mrs. Ralph Ephraim, Mrs. Israel Dorman, Mr. and Mrs. Sidney Schiff, Mr. and Mrs. Edwin Fleishmann, Dr. and Mrs. Sylvan Rosenheim, Mr. and Mrs. Samuel Fisher, Mr. Julius Wyman, Mr. Albert Berney, Mr. and Mrs. Harry Mayer and Nathan Hamburger.

A people used to adversity, driven by an ancient need to continue a journey from darkness to light, made the best of it. Survived, somehow. Far from collective mourning for what they did not have, there appeared to be an ongoing celebration of what they did. On December 22, 1929, less than two months after the stock market crash, Beth Tfiloh marked the eighth anniversary of its founding (and again in 1936, a weeklong celebration of its fifteenth anniversary). On February 28, 1932, the Ohel Yakov congregation celebrated its fiftieth anniversary with a banquet in Community Hall at Liberty Heights and Gwynn Oak Avenues, Depression or no Depression. On January 10, 1930, ceremonies were held in Oheb Shalom to celebrate the dedication of an organ—no small gift!—in memory of William Benesch, from his widow.

On April 2, 1937, Har Sinai acquired the former Maryland Country Club at Strathmore and Park Heights Avenues and, the following year, still in the heart of the Depression, moved its expanded Hebrew school to this "uptown" location. That same April, Beth Jacob held its first service in the Sunnyside School at 5711 Park Heights Avenue. And in January 1932, Shaarei Zion celebrated its thirteenth anniversary and installed Israel Tabak as its spiritual leader.

The Depression of the 1930s—the wiped-out savings, the scrambling for jobs, the scrounging for rent, the struggle to maintain synagogue life—is now the stuff of *bubbe meises*, or grandmother stories. But observing the easier money of later years, those who remember what it was like to be Jewish in Baltimore in the 1930s may be forgiven for remembering the difference.

Originally published in two parts, "Hard Times, Shattered Dreams," March 28, 2003, and "Game of Survival," April 25, 2003.

Before the War: The Class of 1941

On the night of March 20, 1940, about 150 teenage couples were dancing to the music of one of America's most popular dance bands of the era, Eddie Duchin and His Orchestra, in the gym of Forest Park High School, at Chatham Road and Eldorado Avenue.

The gym was decorated with flowing ribbons of crepe paper in the school colors of green and gray. Lights and music were kept soft; faculty chaperones, unobtrusive. The couples danced slowly and closely to such pop tunes as "I'll Never Smile Again" by Frank Sinatra and also much faster and apart, jitterbugging to Glenn Miller's "Tuxedo Junction." Dressed in cashmere sweaters, bobby sox and saddle shoes, they danced as if there would be no tomorrow. But for this class, tomorrow came soon enough: the dance would turn out to be both the highlight of its spring festival, the Jolly Junior Jubilee, and a souvenir of the high-school days of the last generation in Jewish Baltimore to graduate "before the war."

War broke out the following December, making theirs the first class in a generation to be torn apart by war, to see families scattered, careers derailed, boyfriends distanced, marriages postponed and couples bearing for a lifetime the scars of war.

Sixty-seven years after that night, eleven of those same girls, now grandmothers and great-grandmothers, enjoyed lunch in the Artful Gourmet restaurant in Owings Mills. They remembered that long-ago, sugarplum world of high school in Baltimore in the 1940s and what happened to their lives later on. They counted among them about fifty grandchildren, as

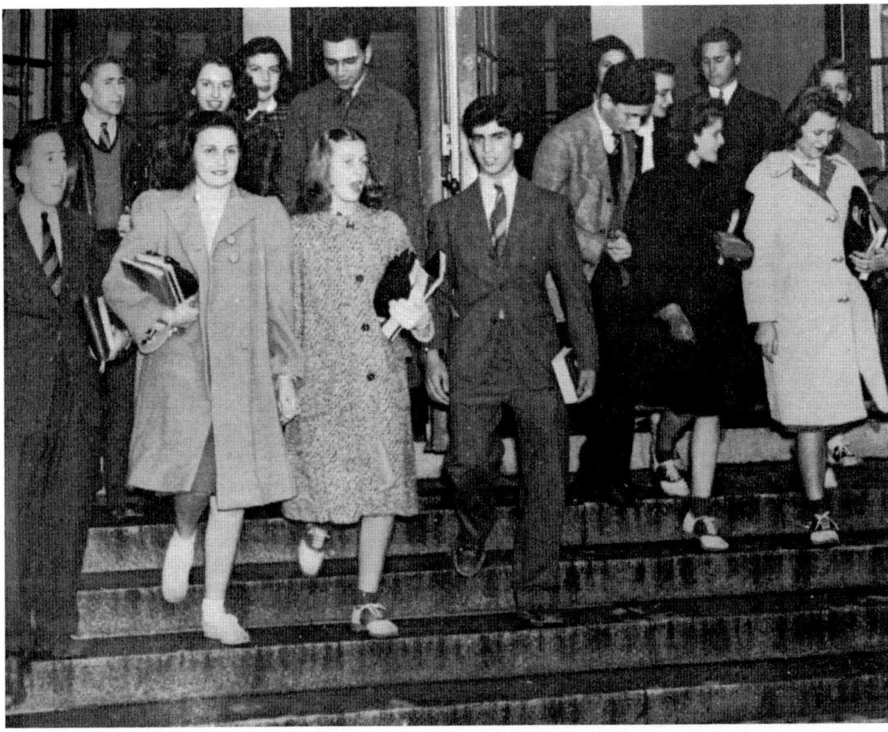

Saddle-shoed students on the school steps pictured in the *Forester*, February 1940. *Gift of Michael Oppenheim, 1995.96.2.*

many as twenty-five great-grandchildren, four divorces and several second marriages. None was in a wheelchair; only one carried a cane.

It is said that in Baltimore social circles, when asked what school one went to, the questioner doesn't mean what college but what high school. Forest Park was among the four public high schools in Baltimore that Jewish boys and girls attended through the 1950s. There were also City College (an all-boys high school), the oldest and perhaps the most prestigious; Poly (all boys, all bent on careers in engineering); Western (all girls); and Forest Park, which was coed (which may account for its popularity). This is a story of what happened to one particular class of Forest Park—the class of 1941 that came out of the Great Depression and inherited the war years in Jewish Baltimore.

How were their lives—their courtships, careers and marriages—shaped by the special time they lived through, a mix of the dating scene and the uncertainties of a war? Herewith, freighted with dreams both broken and fulfilled, are eleven profiles.

Recalls Sonia Fox Schnaper: "Dating in those war years for our class was so different from the classes before us. We were the first to find that all of our dates were soldiers. I'd get calls from soldiers at Aberdeen and Fort Meade—they always seemed to have some connection to your family. Every Sunday we went down to the USO in the YMHA on Monument Street for dances and dinners. And yes, I do remember the night Eddie Duchin played at Forest Park. You know, we didn't have dates—we girls just came and danced!" She met her future husband, Iz Schnaper, in 1946 and married him in 1947. She is widowed.

Helene Tucker Land remembers: "I was part of that prewar dating scene—movies at the Century and the Valencia, afterwards a bite at Nates and Leons, or the A&W Hot Shoppe at Carlin's Park. Most all the guys in our class were called up into the armed services. We dated the soldiers and sailors who happened to be in Baltimore." In 1947, after a three-year absence from her high school sweetheart, Norman Land, who was in the army overseas, she married him. She is also widowed.

Evelyn Wasserman Berman was drawn to the school's art program, under the direction of Nellie Norris. "I spent my entire time at Forest Park in that program," she said. Ms. Berman went on to the University of Maryland and found that most of the male students were in either the Army or Navy or on deferments. She met her future husband, Sid Berman, after the war. "We got married June 1947 and were married twenty-four years, when I was widowed. My life's work started when I became an arts major in Forest Park."

In 1939, while a student at Forest Park, Miriam Dorf met her music teacher, Genevieve Butler, who inspired Miriam's lifetime career in music. While attending Goucher College, she met Marine Lieutenant Bernard Poliakoff. "Bernard and I got engaged in 1943," she said, "just before he had volunteered for a mission so secret that to this day, sixty years later, we still don't have a complete understanding of it. He came home, and we got married. We had one son. Bernard later committed suicide. The war had broken him."

The war would also have a profound effect on the life of Shirley Kirsh Blum:

> *In 1943, I married Bernie Blum, while he was in the army. He left for overseas shortly afterward. When he came home in 1946, he was not the same guy. He had seen too much war in Italy and North Africa. He was taken prisoner and lived out the war in Stalag 17. He limped from shrapnel in his leg, and he was depressed from his prison experience. He died in 1970, when he was only forty-seven. The year 1941 was not the best of times to have graduated high school.*

Shirley Kolodner Sachs got married about a year and a half after graduating Forest Park in 1941:

> *This was wartime. We knew my fiancé, Paul, would be called up soon, so we got married. We lived with my parents. Marrying and living with parents, waiting until boyfriends and husbands came home, well, many couples were doing that during the war. Paul was drafted, I continued at Towson State Teachers College. He was in the battle of Saipan, and was away two years. If I hadn't graduated in 1941 as war was breaking out, our lives would have been quite different.*

For Sylvia Berkow Finkelstein, graduating into the world at war changed both her working life and her social life. She was employed at the U.S. Department of Transportation, which arranged to send celebrities overseas to entertain the servicemen. "I looked up from my desk one day, and there was Al Jolson! Clark Gable came in a few days later," she said. "It was exciting work." Weekends and some evenings, Sylvia went to the USO at the YMHA on Monument Street. "I met a soldier there from North Carolina, and as young people will do so quickly in wartime, we fell in love. We corresponded—and then the mail stopped. I learned that he had been killed on the beach at Normandy." She was married forty-eight years to William Finkelstein before they divorced.

Shortly after Selma Loewner Pleet graduated Forest Park in 1941, she met the young man who would be her husband, Jerry (who would become Dr. Jerry Pleet), and then went to work for the War Department in Washington. The war separated them: Jerry was soon in the army in Louisiana, and although Selma joined him there on at least one occasion, they were apart for most of those years—until April 1945, when they got married. "It was different for the class of 1941," she says. "The war changed our lives. But—we survived!" And so has the Pleets's marriage.

Elaine Gottesman Fedder married Herbert Fedder (whom she had met about a year earlier) in 1943, when he was in the United States Army Air Corps:

> *Like so many of us in those wartime days, we were both swept off of our feet and we got married. Married life during the war was different. Many of us moved to the base where our husbands were stationed, and that is what I did. I moved to an apartment near the base at Monroe, Louisiana, and we lived that way until the war ended. There was a small Jewish*

community and we were both active in it. It was not a bad life at the time, but it was the only life in those years.

Mrs. Fedder and her husband divorced in 1973.

Leslie Tregor Easton's family moved to Washington six months before she was scheduled to graduate. So to stay with her class, she moved in with Baltimore friends:

I took my boyfriend, Ralph Easton, to my prom, and when the war broke out six months later, he enlisted in the Army Air Corps. He was sent to a base in Wichita Falls, Texas, and like so many girls in the Class of 1941, I followed him, and we got married there. We lived there for two years, and then Ralph was sent to the China-Burma-India theater. I came back to Baltimore and stayed with my mother and two sisters, both of whose husbands were also overseas. Fortunately, Ralph came back, safe and well. We had four children; we have been married sixty-five years. Graduating in the Class of 1941 in wartime changed our lives forever. Happily, it all worked out.

Beatrice Gold Lazarus graduated out of the commercial course and, with the country moving to a war footing, went to work in the burgeoning Glenn L. Martin plant in Middle River. She met and, in 1942, married Murray Lazarus:

It was not long before Murray was drafted into the army. He was sent first to Washington state, and I followed him and lived near the bases to be with him. But the time came, and he was sent overseas—Australia, the Philippines, New Guinea.

When that happened, I moved back home with my parents in the house I was born and raised in, on Oakley Avenue in Pimlico. Murray was on the way to Japan when Truman dropped the bomb, and the war was over, and he came home. We had two children. Murray died eleven years ago. The war disrupted our lives. It was difficult for us, but we were lucky to have gotten through it all the way that we did.

But back to that lunch at the Artful Gourmet in Owings Mills. After coffee and dessert and more exchanges of reminiscences about high school days and nights and reunions over the years, Sonia Schnaper, acting as chairperson, clinked a glass and made an announcement. "All right girls, let's talk about the *next* reunion. October 21? How many plan to attend?" Every hand went up—in memory of Eddie Duchin, and the gym that long-ago night decorated in green and gray and the war that changed everything for the girls in the Forest Park High Class of 1941.

Originally published as "Class Spirit," October 26, 2007.

Demonstrators: Baltimore Rabbis Confront Segregation

Awakening on the morning of February 8, 1962, the Jews of Baltimore were stunned to see in their morning newspaper a two-column picture that, for the Baltimore Jewish community, would close one era and open another. The picture would please some, disturb others and become the talk of the synagogue circuit. The caption beneath the picture described the event depicted:

> *Demonstrators: Five clergy and the Urban League director stand outside segregated restaurant that refused to serve them. They are from left: Rabbi Abraham Shaw, Rev. Fred M. Webber, Rev. Joseph Connelly, Rabbi Morris Lieberman, Rabbi Abraham Shusterman, and Dr. Furman Templeton.*

Although Webber, Connelly and Templeton may have been unfamiliar to Jewish readers, the rabbis were not: Rabbi Shaw was the longtime spiritual leader of Temple Oheb Shalom, Rabbi Lieberman of Baltimore Hebrew Congregation and Rabbi Shusterman of Har Sinai. Whatever the arguments in support of the rabbis within the Jewish community, or whatever murmurs of dissent, the fact of the matter was that the scene marked a breakthrough in Jewish social action. In terms of visibility and intensity, nothing like it had ever occurred in the Jewish community before. In one confrontational moment at the door of Miller Brothers restaurant on that long-ago day, the three prominent rabbis gave new definition to their roles.

Rabbis Lieberman, Shaw and Shusterman knew full well that their actions would attract citywide attention and force their respective congregations to ponder the vexing problem of just how far rabbinic leadership should go with social activism as preached from their respective pulpits. Rabbi Lieberman said that the demonstration was adopted "wholeheartedly by all the clergymen as a joint project." At the time, the Maryland General Assembly was considering equal accommodations legislation, though the outcome was still uncertain.

The two targeted restaurants were Miller Brothers and Mandell-Ballow. Knowing the segregation policies of the restaurants and, for that matter, the seething racial climate at the time, the rabbis—in the company of Dr. Templeton, an African American—presented themselves at each restaurant. Both had been picketed by biracial groups of students in previous weeks after they were refused service. The students had gone to the restaurants unannounced. In contrast, before starting their demonstrations, the clerical

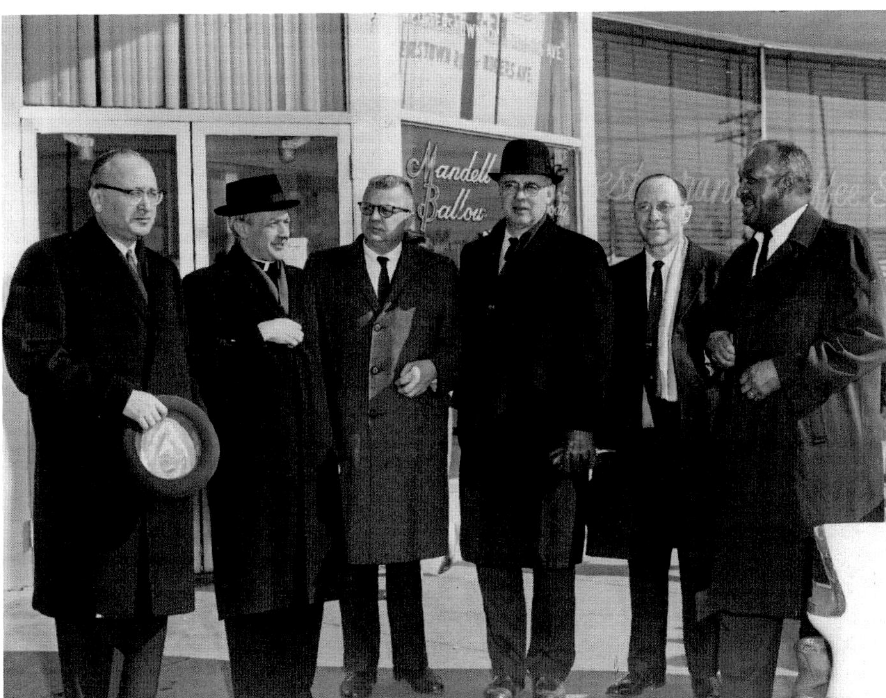

Clergyman take a stand outside the Mandell-Ballow restaurant at Reisterstown and Rogers Avenue, February 1962. *Courtesy of the University of Maryland Libraries, Special Collections and the Hearst Corporation, CP 4.2012.4.*

group telephoned ahead to inform the restaurants of their plans. Dr. Templeton said, "This was done to give the restaurants every advantage. The two restaurants were selected at random from any number we could have gone to."

The Jewish clergymen, with Dr. Templeton, went first to Mandell-Ballow, at 5435 Reisterstown Road, where they were seated in a crowded dining room. They stayed for a half-hour lunch. "Nobody gave us a second look," Dr. Templeton said. "Several people came over to talk to us." Benjamin H. Roffman, comptroller of the restaurant, told reporters that Mandell-Ballow favored a public accommodations bill that would require all restaurants to serve African Americans. But he said the restaurant would remain segregated until the bill passed. "We served the group out of deference to the clergymen. The issue can't be resolved on the sidewalk in front of Mandell-Ballow. It's got to be taken care of in Annapolis."

Shortly after, the group presented itself to the maitre d' at the door of Miller's and asked to be seated. The request was refused. The maitre d' said, simply and matter-of-factly, "We are not integrated."

On being refused entrance, Rabbi Lieberman, speaking for the group, told reporters present (the press had been informed of the time and place of the confrontation), "The idea of the demonstration grew out of a meeting last week of the rabbis and Dr. Templeton. We felt it necessary to make a witness of support for an equal accommodations law. It was our desire to do what we could to advance the progress of the law by showing that our convictions in this matter grew out of religious teaching and to show that this is a subject of concern to a widespread section of the community."

Some in the community were not surprised to see the confrontation. Rabbi Lieberman had advised his board at an earlier meeting of his intention

> *to participate in a course of action agreed upon by the Baltimore Board of Rabbis as protest against racial discrimination and in support of the pending equal accommodations legislation. A group of Christian clergymen and rabbis will meet in the next few days to discuss plans on a joint basis for conveying to the restaurant owners association their interest in the passage of the equal accommodations bill and their intention to urge a boycott of all restaurants which persist in discrimination should the bill fail. Rabbi Lieberman, Rabbi Shaw and Rabbi Shusterman, and perhaps other clergymen and Dr. Templeton, director of the Urban League, will attempt to be served at two restaurants—one of which will be Jewish. Advance notice of this has been given to the press.*

When the news broke that morning of February 8, 1962, sentiment for and against the rabbis' actions in the community was split. Martin Dannenberg was president of Har Sinai at the time. He recalled the episode:

> *When I saw the picture in the* Sun, *I was surprised. Rabbi Shusterman and I had not discussed it. But I took for granted that my own view represented the majority of the Har Sinai Congregation when I sent Rabbi Shusterman a telegram immediately. In it I acknowledged the officers' and board's approval of his actions and pledged the support of the congregation. It is true, I did hear from some members who disapproved, some mildly, some with strong feelings against it. They said things like, "Rabbis should not be doing things like that."*

The congregations involved, however, generally supported their rabbis.

The rabbis' confrontation at Miller Brothers did not happen in a vacuum. Arguably, it was simply one important event in a continuum of Jewish activism in Baltimore's civil rights movement. An even more dramatic show of rabbinic activism in the Baltimore civil rights movement would occur less than a year and a half later—when rabbis were a presence in the historic confrontation at Gwynn Oak Park.

Fourth of July 1963 started out like many a Fourth in Baltimore. The weather was a cool and pleasant seventy-eight degrees. There were parades, cookouts, ball games, fireworks and speeches scheduled all over town. That evening, the city would put on its own mammoth fireworks display at Memorial Stadium. Baltimore was on holiday. But not everybody was taking the holiday. Before this day was over, Baltimore would be a changed city.

Around noon, about four hundred people assembled at the Metropolitan United Methodist Church at 1121 West Lanvale Street. This was no ordinary gathering: the assemblage included respected and widely known clergymen, both local and national, white and black, young and old, Catholic, Protestant and Jewish. Reverend William Sloan Coffin, chaplain of Yale; Monsignor Austin J. Healy; and Reverend Marion C. Bascom were among those assembled. The group also included Reform Rabbis Morris Lieberman of the Baltimore Hebrew Congregation, Samuel Glasner of Temple Emanuel and Philip Schecter of Temple Oheb Shalom, as well as Conservative Rabbi Israel Goldman of Chizuk Amuno. They were there to help in the organization of a protest march on Gwynn Oak Park, the popular Baltimore amusement park, which had produced controversy for years because of its "white only" admissions policy.

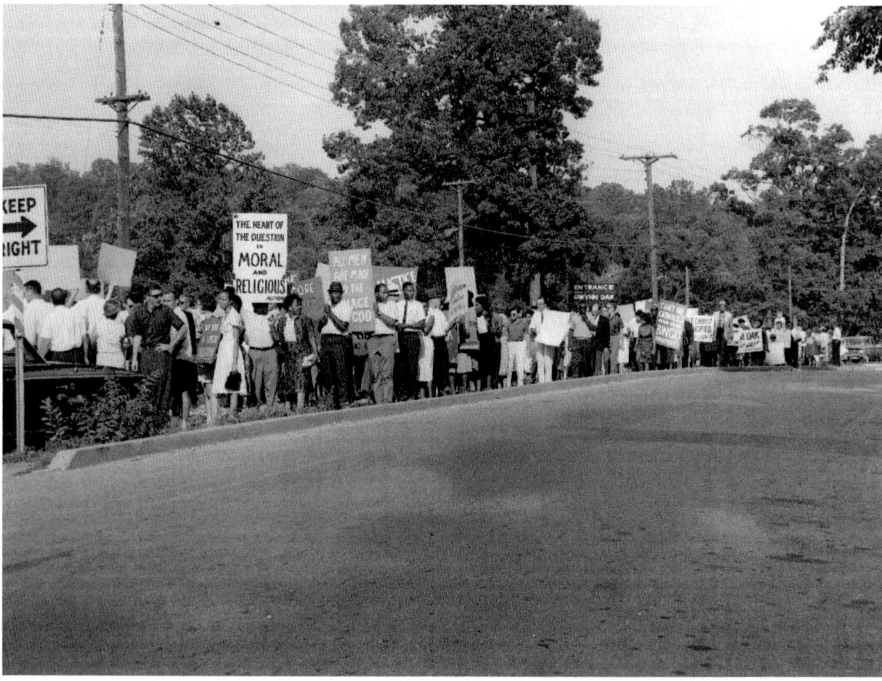

Demonstrators line up outside the entrance of Gwynn Oak Amusement Park to protest racial segregation, July 1963. *Courtesy of the University of Maryland Libraries, Special Collections and the Hearst Corporation, CP 4.2012.3.*

The group discussed how the protest was to be carried out (peacefully), and whether participants were willing, individually or together, to go to jail (yes). At 1:30 p.m., the group made its way out of the church, marching arm-in-arm and singing, "We shall overcome, We shall overcome, We shall overcome some day-a-a-ay." They boarded buses and headed west for Gwynn Oak Park—for a confrontation with Baltimore County Police and a rendezvous with history.

It was about 3:00 p.m. when the protesters arrived at the main gate. They crowded the gate, only to be met by Chief Robert Lally of the Baltimore County Police and, behind him, fifty policemen. (Lally would reveal later that police dogs, though not visible, were kept on call, along with several hundred additional policemen.) As more buses arrived, the protesters joined a marching picket line on the median strip on Gwynn Oak Avenue in front of the park.

The focus of interest soon became the main gate, where Chief Lally and his police cordon blocked protesters. Lally read the Maryland Trespass Act,

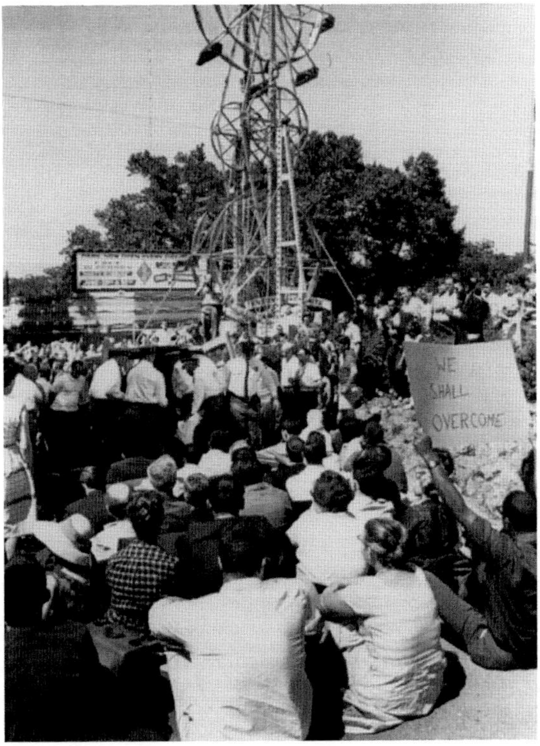

"Police arrested wave after wave of White and Negro demonstrators protesting racial segregation at suburban Gwynn Oak Amusement Park. Police reported at least 223 persons had been arrested. As demonstrators sit in the foreground, police carry their colleagues to patrol wagons and buses." Baltimore News American, *July 5, 1963. Courtesy of the University of Maryland Libraries, Special Collections and the Hearst Corporation, CP 4.2012.5.*

charged the protesters with violating it and ordered them arrested. Obviously embarrassed at having to lock up so many clergymen, he said, "As chief of police I have no alternative. The law of Maryland says they can't trespass. I can't legislate."

Quietly, orderly and to the accompaniment of freedom songs, the protesters complied, peacefully, all 283 of them. They boarded the county school buses that Lally had ready for them and were driven off to the Woodlawn police station. A young lawyer named Robert Watts, who later became Judge Watts, met them to act as counsel.

The entire protest was peaceful—in the picket line, at the gate, on the buses and in the police station. Incidents of harassment were few. There were no reports of the police brutality that had marked similar protests throughout the country in those years. "The police," said Reverend Joseph Connolly of St. Bernadette's Roman Catholic Church, "were very gracious." Rabbis Glasner and Goldman were fingerprinted and photographed in a makeshift jail at the Pikesville Armory. Rabbi Goldman later remarked of the episode, "It has been the most dramatic experience of my life." Rabbi

Lieberman, released on bail, smiled when he was asked why he had joined the demonstration. He said, "I think every American should celebrate the Fourth of July."

The president of Baltimore Hebrew Congregation at the time was Samuel "Sandy" Frank. He recalled:

> *Rabbi Lieberman did not announce to the congregation that he planned to help organize the clergy and march with them in the protest, nor did he in the weeks following see the need to "explain" himself. However, he sermonized about it, although he had the sense that some of the congregants disapproved of what he was doing. After all, there is, then and now, a question of just how far into social action our rabbinate should go. I do know from my personal experience that some congregants were upset. You know, "Rabbis shouldn't be doing this sort of thing." But they did not make their discontent with Rabbi Lieberman's actions known in any formal way.*

E.B. Hirsh was active in the Baltimore Hebrew Congregation at the time and remembered the genesis of Rabbi Lieberman's activism:

> *After World War II, Rabbi Lieberman brought together a number of young people in the congregation to discuss the issues of the times. Civil rights was one of those issues. He did bring it up often, and he did encourage discussion about the movement. It seems to me that he wasn't keen on the idea of demonstration but I remember his saying that sometimes "you have to put your body where your mouth is." So those of us in the group were not at all surprised to see him taking the lead in the Gwynn Oak demonstration. This was in the early days of the Jewish community's social activism, and I think we were among the first congregations in America to take up the cause of civil rights. The group included Lou and Dorrie Fox, Irv and Lois Blum, Sandy and Carole Frank, Marty and Marge Robbins, Chuck and Alice Hoffberger, Nancy and Larry Katz.*
>
> *But opinion in the congregation was split. Some prominent members were absolutely against the idea of highly visible community action. But Rabbi Lieberman dealt with them and did what he thought he had to do.*

Following the protest, the *Jewish Times* editorialized:

> *Although some in the Jewish community would be quick to criticize the action of our rabbis and other clergymen because of the abrogation of*

antiquated "trespass laws" those who can differentiate between right and wrong are quick to realize that the cause for which our rabbis are fighting is a just cause—a cause which demands the support not only of clergymen of all faiths but the rank and file of our citizenry.

Many, in the days and weeks that followed, would say that the protest had been effective, that the issue of integration of public accommodations was resolved. In fact, the park was integrated late in August of that same year, when Spiro Agnew, then the Baltimore County Executive, persuaded the county council to create a Human Relations Commission that opened Gwynn Oak to all. In 1974, with changing tastes and changing times, the park was closed.

But that day, largely forgotten by the Baltimore Jewish community, remains a highly visible and vivid remembrance of Baltimore's rabbis taking action that helped change the history of Baltimore.

Originally published in two parts, "Longing to Overcome," February 22, 2002, and "Stand at Gwynn Oak," March 22, 2002.

PART 3

Earning a Living

Barred from many professions in the Old World, many Jewish newcomers arrived in America with one finely honed business skill: commerce. As peddlers, traders, shopkeepers and the like, European Jews came equipped to benefit from a burgeoning American economy. Most started out small, barely making ends meet, building businesses to support their families. A few newcomers made it big, especially in the needle trades, wholesaling and retail, most notably the founders of the great department stores of downtown Baltimore.

New arrivals found employment in a variety of trades. In these stories of work life, we encounter midwives and salesmen, grocery owners and pharmacists. What they had in common was that many worked in family businesses in which everyone pitched in to keep things going. Many in the second and third generations were able to make their way into larger businesses and the professions, but a lot of Baltimore Jews can still recall their early years in modest family enterprises.

What's Brewing?

The young couple and their babe-in-arms were among the countless faces in a surge of disembarking immigrants jostling for position behind a guard rail, waiting to be cleared by an immigration officer, on the churning, noisy Pier Eight, Locust Point, in South Baltimore. The tag on the lapel of the man read, "Charles Hohberger"—and we have the word of Sara Feldman, granddaughter of Abe Hoffberger, that the immigration officer changed "Hohberger" to "Hoffberger." Charles was twenty-five. The tag on the lady, Charles's wife, read "Sarah." She was either fifteen or twenty (depending on which census you choose to believe). Abe was the one-year-old babe-in-arms. The year was 1882.

The little family had made their way from the town of Bobova or some other village in the province of Galicia (depending on the account you choose to believe), villages at the time in Austria-Hungary and now a part of southern Poland, to the German port city of Bremen. There they were herded aboard a ship of the North German Lloyd line, bound for Baltimore. They sailed in steerage.

Fourteen days later, they docked in Baltimore. Disembarking, they found their way to East Baltimore, to a tiny residence at 1106 Low Street, across the street from Sarah's mother, Mollie. Lois Hoffberger Feinblatt, the daughter of Sam and Gertrude Miller Hoffberger, says, "How Mollie got to this country and exactly when, and got to be living in her own house on Low Street, we don't know. We didn't think to ask them the right questions while they lived. And now we will never know."

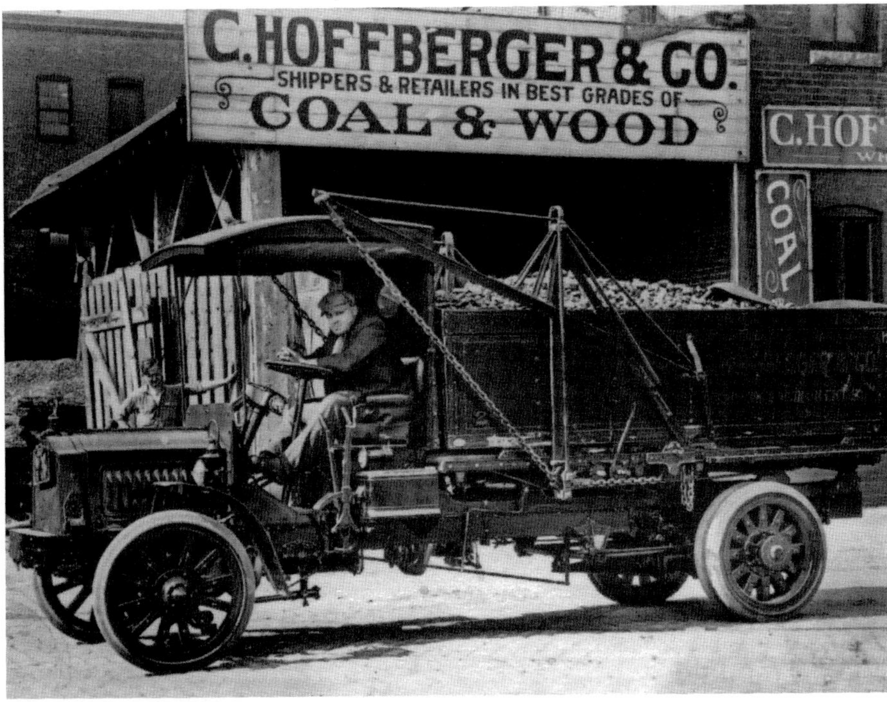

The Hoffberger family, perhaps best known for their days of brewing beer and owning the Baltimore Orioles in the late 1960s and through the 1970s, had humble beginnings. Charles Hoffberger, the family patriarch, began his success by selling wood, coal and ice in Baltimore City. *Gift of Charles Hoffberger, 1994.124.1.*

What we do know is that in 1896, the Ohel Yaakov synagogue moved from 610 Forest Street to 1164 Low Street, the same block where the Hoffbergers were living. The oral history of the family holds that, given the proximity of Ohel Yaakov at the time, Charles and Sarah Hoffberger were members of Ohel Yaakov until each died, Charles in 1907 and Sarah in 1925. When Sarah died, Eunice, the daughter of Abe and Lena Hoffberger, recalled, "The funeral procession stopped in different places that Sarah had known. When they came to the synagogue [then at 613 Aisquith Street] the doors were held open wide."

We also know that Charles did not become a tailor in one of the many Baltimore clothing factories, as so many of his fellow immigrants did. He began dealing in the sale and delivery of ice and milk, coal and wood—and successfully. Over the years, the family's business interests would include Merchants Terminal, Baltimore Transfer, Pompeian Olive Oil, Abbots Bitters, Solarine Wax and, in 1931, when the family bought a little-known brewery, producing an obscure beer called National Bohemian.

National Bohemian Beer traces its origins through a tangled history to the old Baltimore brewery known as Gottleib-Baurenschmidt-Straus (GBS), which flourished locally until Prohibition began in 1919. At that point, beer officially disappeared and did not reappear until Prohibition's repeal in 1933. A few years earlier, undoubtedly anticipating repeal, the Hoffberger family had bought GBS, and along with it, the rights to the name and product, National Bohemian Beer.

Jerold C. "Jerry" Hoffberger, son of Gertrude and Sam Hoffberger, who later became chairman of the company, recalled that they brought on board brewmaster Karl Kreitler and hired Arthur Deute as president. "Deute," Jerry Hoffbergerer said, "was a marketing genius. It was his one-eyed "Mr. Boh" who would become the star of so many television commercials, and who sang and danced his way into Baltimore history." But all of that was still to come.

National Bohemian Beer started out as one of a half dozen or so locally brewed beers competing for Baltimore's historic taste for suds. Local brewers

The iconic "Mr. Boh," seen here, was introduced in 1936 and has remained popular even after his retirement in the 1960s. Some consider Natty Boh to be the unofficial mascot of Baltimore City. *Gift of David Hoffberger, 1999.129.5.*

had been at it since the 1740s, when breweries thrived in the Belair Road, West Baltimore and Canton sections. Early brands included Steil's, Bech's, Clagett's, Staub's, Brehm's and, later, Weisner's, Free State, Gunther, American and Arrow—names that would dominate the market into the 1950s. National had yet to mount a serious challenge.

Fortunately for Mr. Boh, the company was looking to expand, coinciding with the time that television, with its endless potential for entertaining and persuading, was exploding onto the media scene. Said Jerry Hoffberger: "With imaginative guidance from the W.B. Doner advertising agency, Mr Boh became a fixture on Baltimore TV, largely through the presence of Chuck Thompson, Jim McManus [later Jim McKay] of ABC, Bailey Goss and of course Mr. Boh himself." National quickly jumped into sponsorship of the Baltimore Orioles, Washington Senators and Baltimore Colts.

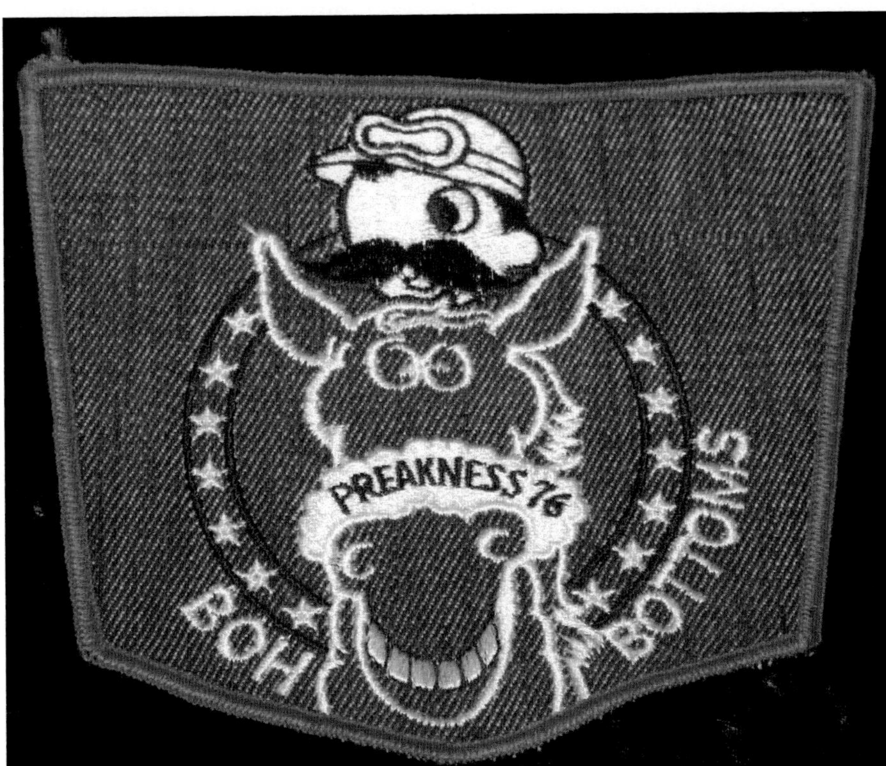

The Preakness Stakes and National Bohemian beer have been Baltimore staples since the late 1800s. Here we see those two Baltimore icons brought together on this 1976 denim patch. *Gift of the Hoffberger Family, 2007.54.10.*

The big breakthrough came unexpectedly, five thousand feet in the air over the Chesapeake Bay. "Early in the 1950s," said Mr. Hoffberger, "several executives—Dawson Farber, Sydney Marcus and I, all from National Beer, and "Brod" Doner and Herb Fried from our ad agency—had just taken off in a private plane from Logan Field. We were soaring high over the Bay and looking down on its shorelines on a brilliant, sunlit day. I said, 'What a gorgeous sight!' Doner picked up on that. He said, 'This place is the land of pleasant living.'" That phrase became National Bohemian Beer's slogan for the next thirty years and the credo for a "land" that stretched from Ocean City to Deep Creek Lake.

The rest of this story makes up the history not just of the Hoffbergers and National Bohemian Beer but also of the Baltimore region itself. From the 1950s well into the 1970s, Baltimore happily equated its love for National Bohemian Beer with civic pride. We said we were from the land of pleasant living and snapped out to bartenders, "Make mine a Natty Boh!" "Boh" had become part of the Baltimore patois. No city could have been more in love with its beer than Baltimore was with National Bohemian.

The Hoffberger legacy has been, first, the enrichment of Baltimore's philanthropy and, second, the shaping of the region's pop culture. Mr. Boh turned out to be more than a simple advertising icon. He became a lovable troubadour, soothing us with his singing and dancing, his words and his music, creating just the playful mood the city needed to deal with the challenge of stumbling out of one era, the 1940s, into another, the 1950s, exchanging its heavy industry for light, in a losing swap.

And so it was that for thirty uncertain years, in a time when Baltimoreans had reason not to feel good about their city, they did—led by Mr. Boh's merry cheerleading:

National Beer, National Beer
We'll sing you a song of National Beer
And while we're singing I'm here to say
It's brewed on the shores of the Chesapeake Bay.

For Baltimoreans looking back through the gossamer of years, the Hoffbergers were giving us more than a jingle. They were playing our song.

Originally published as "What's Brewing," October 27, 2006.

The Midwives of Old East Baltimore

On the spring night of June 8, 1917, a loud knocking at the door of Fannie Silberman, of 828 East Baltimore Street, brought her awake. Mrs. Silberman was a midwife, one of as many as twenty-five (depending on the year) delivering babies in the Jewish neighborhoods of East Baltimore in the late 1800s and early 1900s. She was used to midnight callers, and she knew the drill: quickly, she dressed, woke her husband, grabbed a medical bag and rushed to the door, to be greeted, this time, by a nervous teenager. He blurted, "Annie Goldman!"

Ordinarily, by this time in this oft-played drama, Fannie's husband, Louis, had hitched up his horse and wagon and was ready to chauffeur Fannie to the patient. But in this case, the mother-in-labor was only eight houses away, at 812 East Baltimore Street. Mrs. Silberman took charge. She said to the boy, "Go!" They did, at a brisk walk, half a block down the street to the west.

This scene of haste, urgency and rushing about through the night was enacted dozens of times in the East Baltimore of the early 1900s and among this same population as late as the mid-1920s as it began to resettle in Northwest Baltimore. Written records, scarce as they are, and more abundantly, the *bubbe meises* ("grandmother tales"), make clear why the midwives, in that time and place, were so busy. Most of the Jews did not use the doctors and facilities at then-nearby Sinai Hospital. In 1922, only 22 percent of births in Baltimore were in hospitals, and the percentage of Jews giving births in hospitals was even lower.

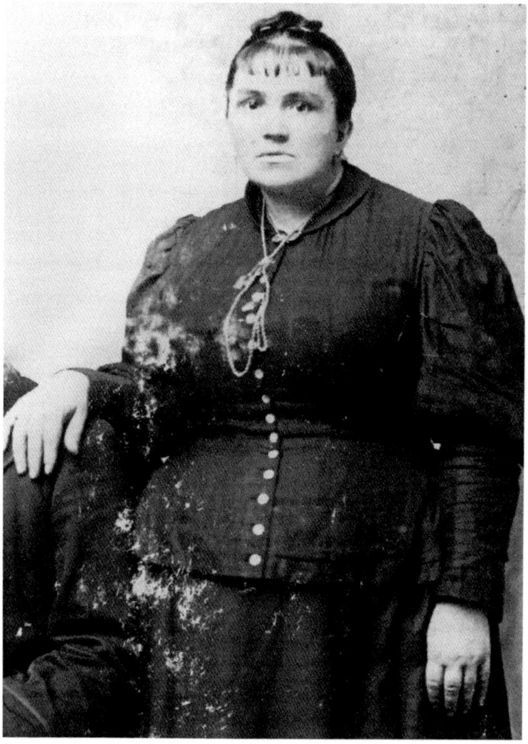

Rosa Feinberg is said to have delivered two thousand babies over the course of her thirty-six years as a Baltimore midwife. While this number may be an exaggeration, she was certainly kept busy—for twenty-five dollars, Rosa not only delivered the baby but also spent the following week caring for newborn and mother alike. *Gift of Pearl Began, 1966.3.33.*

Mrs. Peggy Engel Frankel and Mrs. Pat Goldiner Statter, granddaughters of Fannie Silberman, recall their grandmother's explanation. Mrs. Frankel says, "She told us that these immigrants, recently removed from the *shtetls* of Eastern Europe, spoke only Yiddish and were wary of 'authorities' and were accustomed to midwives—it was the way they had their babies delivered in the old country. They did not trust the institutions in Europe, and they didn't trust them here."

An earlier history ("My Grandmother Was A Midwife," Naomi Kellman, *Baltimore Jewish Times,* September, 1982) offered reminiscences by other grandchildren of Jewish midwives in Baltimore. Rosa Feinberg's granddaughter Pearl Began recalled, "She kept a ball of string and every time she delivered a baby she would tie a small knot in it. Before she died, she could count 2,000 knots." Lena Barber "lived at 44 West York Street in South Baltimore and did not use horse and buggy to get to the home of her clients. She walked," recalled granddaughter Rose Kushner. Leonard Harmatz grew up with grandmother Bessie Harmatz. "We lived in the 1100, and then the 1400, block of East Baltimore Street, within walking distance of her patients," he said. "When she couldn't walk there, she took the streetcar. She delivered dozens of babies a year." Among them were the five children of Samuel and Lena Rubenstein Silver, including Edgar, who would become a judge. Louis Isaacs recalled that his grandmother "had a sign outside of her house at 1820 East Baltimore Street, 'Chasyo Isaacs, Registered Midwife.' She would deliver ten and twelve babies in a single family."

Some records of all of those deliveries survive. Here are a few: on December 1, 1910, at the home of Ida and Solomon Shavitz at 700 South Charles Street, a daughter, Lily. Mr. Shavitz was listed as "grocer." On July 13, 1911, to Kolman and Sarah Lapides at 1427 East Baltimore Street, a son, Raymond. Mr. Lapides's occupation was listed as "delicatessen." To the Goldsteins of 620 South Charles Street, a daughter, Lena; to the Kramers of

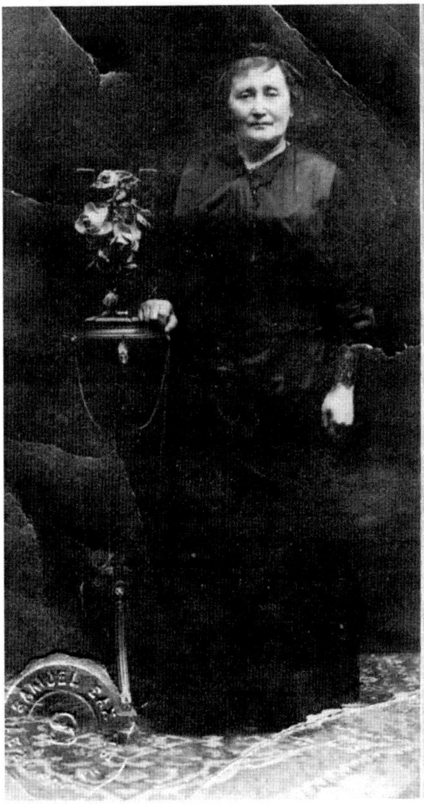

Form 1236

1. Sex Female No. of Child of Mother 10
2. Name of Child Bellah Barber
3. Race or Color White
4. Date May 22 - 1930
5. Place of Birth 3734 Park Heights av
6. Full Name of Mother Esther Barber
7. Mother's Maiden Name Esther Lieberman
8. Mother's Birthplace Russia
9. Full Name of Father Isaac L Barber
10. Father's Occupation Insurance Agent
11. Father's Birthplace Russia

1-27-26—200B.—50L.

Lena Barber, who served Baltimore's mothers from at least 1892 to 1930, maintained copious records, capturing everything from the mother's maiden name to the parents' place of origin. Pictured is Lena at the turn of the century and a record for the birth of one Bella Barber, May 22, 1930. *Gifts of Rose Kushner, 1985.62.1, 2.*

Spring Street, a son, Samuel. In a memoir at the Jewish Museum of Maryland, Mrs. Feinberg's granddaughter, Pearl Began, would recall that Mrs. Barber delivered any number of babies who would grow up and go on to prominence in public life, "including Judge Simon Sobeloff and Bernard Melnicove!"

A few of the midwives were graduates of midwife training programs at the University of Odessa or the Imperial College of Lying In Hospital in Moscow, others simply learned through experience. Many brought with them from the Old Country ancient superstitions: pinning psalms around the mother's bed to ward off the evil eye or putting a Hebrew sign outside the birth house so Lilith (Adam's legendary first wife) wouldn't steal the baby or exchange it for a demon.

Shirley (Mrs. Edwin) Snyder was delivered by a midwife, one of seven of the eight children born to Abraham and Sophia Zusskin Shapiro delivered by midwives. At the time of her birth, the family was living at 4928 Pimlico Road; earlier, they had lived in East Baltimore. She recalls, "My uncle lived with us, and it was his job to keep the children outside while the midwives were at work."

Sarah Liebowitz Miller was delivered by a midwife in 1916, when the family lived on McElderry Street, on a date in January uncertain to this day. The daughter of Haddie Buckman Liebowitz and Morris Liebowitz (who was at one time caretaker of the Workmen's Circle Hall on East Baltimore Street), Mrs. Miller says her real birthday is January 5, but the midwife put down January 9. "Why? Those midwives were so busy they never did know what day it was."

Edith Rosenfeld (Mrs. Sheldon) Tucker recalls that her husband was one of fifteen children of Nathan and Cecelia Tucker, some of whom were delivered by midwives in East Baltimore in the same era: "While all of these fifteen babies were being born," she says, "the Tuckers owned and operated a butcher shop at 1716 East Baltimore Street. I married baby number fourteen."

Samuel "Sam" Levin was delivered by a midwife on April 14, 1930, probably at 3312 Eastern Avenue, the first child born to William and Minnie Weiner Levin: "I didn't know I was delivered by a midwife until in 1960 I got hold of my birth certificate. It read, 'Delivered by Midwife,' and as best as I can read her name, it was 'Silberman.' She lived at 1229 East Baltimore Street. By the way, my mother, Minnie, was well known in East Baltimore; she was a very popular *shochet*."

Ida Rita Rudolph Finkel was delivered by midwife Fannie Silberman on April 16, 1918, where the family lived on Caroline Street. She recalls, "Mrs.

Silberman delivered both of my two sisters and my brother Richard "Dick" Rudolph. My father was a presser at Schoeneman. My mother, coming from Lithuania, was more comfortable having a woman deliver her babies—all of the doctors in those days were men."

But back to the night of June 8, 1917, and Fannie Silberman and the young man racing down the street to Jacob Goldman's, whose wife, Annie, was in labor. It so happens that we know the end of this story: the baby that Annie Goldman delivered that night—her fourth child, a boy—was Daniel Goldman, who at the time of this writing was alive and well and living in Baltimore at 1 Slade Avenue. How did he discover that Fannie Silberman was the midwife who delivered him? Daniel recalls:

> *Growing up, I happened to see among the family things what looked like an old penny postcard. It read, "Jacob and Annie Goldman announce with pride the birth of a son, Daniel, June 8, 1917, seven pounds, three ounces. Midwife, Mrs. Fannie Silberman." That's how I knew that Fannie Silberman delivered me. At some point later in life, I met her granddaughter, Peggy Frankel, and we made the connection. I thanked her for having Fannie as her grandmother, the midwife who brought me into the world, eighty-eight years ago. I thought she did a good job.*

Originally published as "Port of Birth," September 30, 2005.

THE DOWNTOWN WORLD OF THE "CLOAK AND SUITERS"

At precisely 6:30 a.m. on April 3, 1960, Harry Kruger, owner and operator of Kruger's restaurant, put the key in the door of his restaurant at 229 West Baltimore Street, about where the entrance to the Baltimore Civic Center is today. Though he had performed this ritual every morning six days a week for forty years, this day would be different. At the end of it, when he closed his shop, Harry Kruger would be marking a kind of unofficial end to Baltimore's long-dying clothing industry and to the frantic, often colorful life of the men who lived it. These men called themselves "cloak and suiters" in a private jargon they used to describe the brotherhood working in the world of the needle trades.

The manufacture of clothing—men's, women's and children's—flourished in downtown Baltimore, beginning with the Civil War and well up into the 1960s. This industry grew so big, in fact, that Baltimore became a world center of the needle trades. In the earlier years, all of the offices and much of the manufacturing was concentrated in downtown Baltimore. From roughly Paca Street on the west, Fayette Street on the north and a good distance east and south, large factories and smaller lofts and shops turned out everything that could be sewn—men's suits and coats, shirts and ties and ladies dresses, coats and blouses.

The clothing industry included some of the oldest and most-respected names in the history of Jewish Baltimore, for it was in the needle trades that many of these families achieved their wealth and prominence and, in many cases, their positions in the community as leading philanthropists.

Depending on the year, and to name some but surely not all: Abrams and Sons was located at 213 West Redwood Street; Belmont Clothes,

15 West Baltimore Street; S. Ginsberg & Company, 331 West Baltimore Street; H.L. Hartz and Sons, 3 South Hanover Street; B. Katzenstein and Brother, 107 West Fayette Street; Lebow Brothers, 100 West Baltimore Street; Londontown, 311 West Baltimore Street; Louis Marcus, 410 West Lombard Street; A. Schreter and Sons, 16 South Eutaw Street; Max Rubin, 324 West Baltimore Street; Resisto Tie, 40 South Paca Street; A. Sagner and Sons, 32 South Paca Street; J. Schoeneman, Inc., 412 West Redwood Street; Goldman, 38 South Paca; and Wonder Clothes, 124 West Lombard Street.

It was a man's world, harshly competitive, but members of the extended clan gathered amiably, and purposely, for breakfast, lunch and often dinner, in a certain few restaurants located within the field of battle: Kruger's, Globus's, Horn and Horn's, Thompson's and Miller Brothers.

Globus was a tiny hole-in-the-wall cafeteria located in the right times (1930s–50s) and in the right place (Baltimore Street near Eutaw) in the heart of the loft district. Globus had an ambience suggestive of the frenzy in the exit gate at Camden Yards when a game breaks.

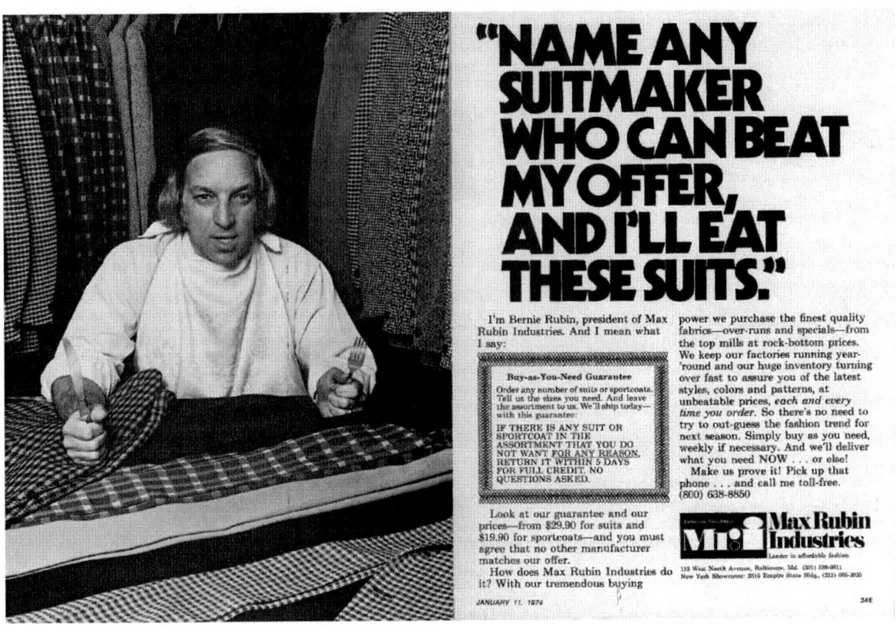

For decades, Baltimore's clothing industry boomed, and anything that could be sewn was made and sold in its garment district. Competition was fierce, but businesses figured out creative ways to stand out from the rest. This advertisement from Max Rubin Industries combines humor with a friendly face. *Gift of Millie Greenberg, 1992.225.68.*

According to Mrs. Shirley Globus Polikoff, who worked there with her mother and brother Ralph, Globus featured delicatessen-style food, roast beef and corned beef, cabbage soup and noodle pudding. "Our biggest seller was potato *latkes*, smothered with sour cream," Polikoff said. "We sold tons of them. Those *latkes* were the staple of the cloak and suiters. They kept those guys alive." Of Globus, Daniel Goldman, who worked a lifetime in the district, commented, "It could get wild in there—what with sewers and cutters and pressers, as well as owners, too, who were drawn to Kosher-style food and the deli-and-East-Baltimore atmosphere."

In contrast to Globus, Kruger's catered more to the many German Jewish clothing executives in the district—of whom there were many, including the Sinsheimers, Kahns, Oppenheimers and Burgunders. According to Joseph Stickell, who worked for Kruger's from 1940 through to the end, "Harry Kruger was a first-class restaurateur, and he catered successfully to the executive class. He kept his restaurant quiet, and his prices high, which is why his customers loved the place."

Horn and Horn, at 304 East Baltimore Street, was home not just to the cloak and suiters, but located as it was so close to the Block, with the Gayety burlesque and its strip clubs, and to city hall and the courthouse, it also attracted a Runyonesque mix of exotic dancers and numbers writers, City Hall types, judges and merchant princes—all sitting side by side. The place was famous too for its remarkable waitresses, who took long and complicated orders from a table of six or so, noting exceptions and special requests without writing any of it down—then delivering it all in perfect order.

Thompson's was on the northwest corner of Fayette and Howard Streets and, given its location in the heart of the department store world, was especially popular with this crowd. Miller Brothers, on Fayette Street between Hanover and Liberty Streets, was a Baltimore institution, and though patronized by the cloak and suiters, its tone and mood were not a part of their world.

The day for many started with breakfast. Patrons would linger over coffee and bagels, a ritual that often phased into a 10:30 a.m. break and a second cup of coffee. Sharing in the gossip were buyers and sellers, shop foremen, cutters, pressers and sewers, all continuing the day's business. The coffee break might drift over into lunch—which for some never ended and became a part of the 3:00 p.m. coffee break, with more business as usual.

Daniel Goldman's family business was the Paramount Clothing Company. The firm manufactured men's suits from 1918 through 1987, with offices and some manufacturing at several locations within the garment district, the last of which was 419 West Redwood.

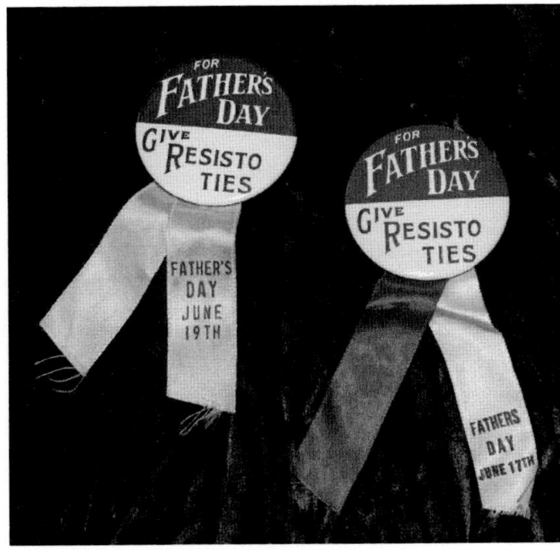

Standing out from the herd was not easy during Baltimore's clothing manufacturing heyday. Resisto Ties, a prominent Baltimore tie maker since 1890, used these flashy buttons as a creative way to advertise its ties as perfect Father's Day gifts. *Museum purchase, 1996.64.2.*

Many alumni of the district look back on the times and think of Henry Frank as the chairman of the board of the whole place. Samuel "Sandy" Frank, the third generation of Franks to own and operate the business of wholesaling fabrics for manufacturing linings, explains: "My father would stake any promising entrepreneur—pressers, cutters, foremen, many of whom had worked for the defunct but once prominent Sonneborn Company. By financing these start-ups he was actually expanding the market for his own product." The firm was started by Aaron Frank, Sandy's grandfather, who migrated to Baltimore from Platz, Germany, in 1841.

But in the fast-changing world of the needle trades, there was no forever. With the impact of overseas (and far more economical) production, the growth of the giant retailers at the expense of the smaller ones and the speed of the changes in men's tastes, the needle trades in Baltimore dwindled and, as a major industry in the city, died a slow death.

Late on that last day, April 3, 1960, a few of the regulars got together in Kruger's to say goodbye to Harry. According to one who was there, they sang a few verses of "For He's a Jolly Good Fellow," and then they all left together. Standing outside, Harry took one last look and locked the door behind him. The occasion must have been particularly poignant, for the old gang surely knew that they were saying farewell to more than a restaurant. They were saying goodbye to the world they knew.

Originally published as "Fabric of Life," September 26, 2001

Gay Street: The Other Howard and Lexington

The Orleans Street Viaduct, as it came to be known, was completed in December 1935, bringing the great retailing names of the Old Town neighborhood into the larger world of Baltimore City. By then, the 300 to 800 blocks of Gay Street were a century-old shopping neighborhood with crowds rivaling Howard and Lexington's.

"Gay Street," as those busy blocks were known, developed serendipitously: in the mid-1800s, they happened to be a wide spot in the road that farmers used, driving their produce in from Maryland and Pennsylvania by way of Belair Road—which is Gay Street extended. They set out their produce for sale in the wide spot—which became Belair Market. By the 1850s, they had erected a market structure, and the wide spot in the road became a busy place to meet friends and to trade.

The timing coincided with the arrival in East Baltimore of Jews from the German-speaking countries of Central Europe. From either Fells Point or Locust Point, they found their way to East Baltimore because that is where the commerce was said to be. As early as 1850, there were Jewish family businesses all over East Baltimore. (An 1850 directory lists Burgunder, Laupheimer, Sinsheimer, Rosenstock, Lazarus, Oppenheimer.) At the market site, seeing the buyers, they set themselves up as sellers. They sold shoes, furniture, dry goods, pots and pans and general merchandise. Over the years, from this tiny family of small German Jewish merchants, emerged at least a dozen mini-department stores that flourished through the mid-1900s.

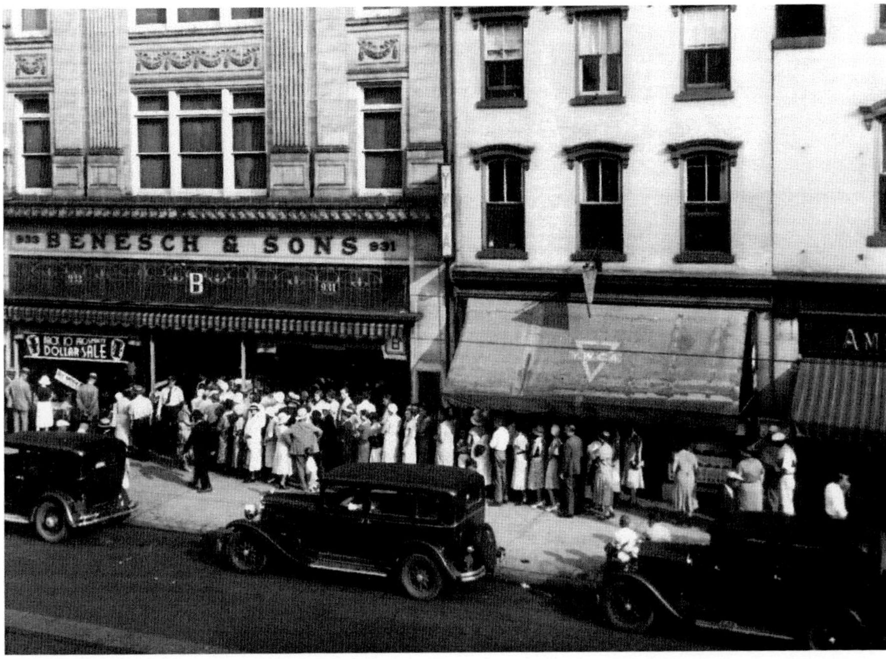

The Great House of Isaac Benesch and Sons had the largest home furnishings department of its time. Established in 1852, the company was one of the first to provide home delivery by gas-powered trucks and to create full-room displays. Here, Baltimoreans line up outside the Gay Street location for a chance at the Dollar Sale, circa 1925. *Gift of Joan Benesch, 2001.120.1.*

Not surprisingly, they opened synagogues in the neighborhood where they both lived and worked: Har Sinai met for the first time in the home of Moses Hutzler at Eastern Avenue and South Exeter Street, about a mile and a half away. Later, as the Jews from Eastern Europe arrived, they opened their own synagogues, including Bikur Cholim, Beth Hamedrash Hagadol and B'nai Israel.

"The Great House of Isaac Benesch" dominated the street. Mr. Benesch came to this country from Prague when he was eight years old and, while still a young man, opened his store on Gay Street in 1852—six years before Hutzler's opened in 1858. But other stores came into business to compete: William Kaufman, Blum's, Irving's, Seif's, Moses Kahn, Silverman's, Epstein's and Bugatch. In between and among them were dozens of smaller stores—shoe stores, jewelry stores and clothing stores. Interestingly, Max Hochschild opened his first store on Gay Street in 1876 (when he was only twenty-one) before he moved to Howard and Lexington Streets with his new partners, Benno and Louis Kohn.

Sam Kotzen went to work at Kaufman's Department Store in 1929 when he was nineteen years old and worked on the street six days a week for seventy-one years, until he retired at ninety in 2000. "Our biggest competition was of course Benesch. They were originally an installment store, sending men out into the neighborhoods to sell furniture and clothing at a dollar down, a dollar a week. But they progressed and became a full-blown retailer."

Marjorie Kahn Golub, the niece of Jerome Kahn of Moses Kahn at Gay and Aisquith, recalls working at the store's office in administration:

> *One of the reasons our store was so widely known was my Uncle Jerome's radio commercials. He wrote them and read them on the air, and his idea was unique—"with each suit, two pair of pants." I think we were among the very first stores to make that offer.*
>
> *Like some other stores on the street, we were a credit store, with men out on the street, and that style of business was one of the big differences between the stores on Gay Street and the Howard and Lexington Street stores. At one time, we had thirty men out on the street.*

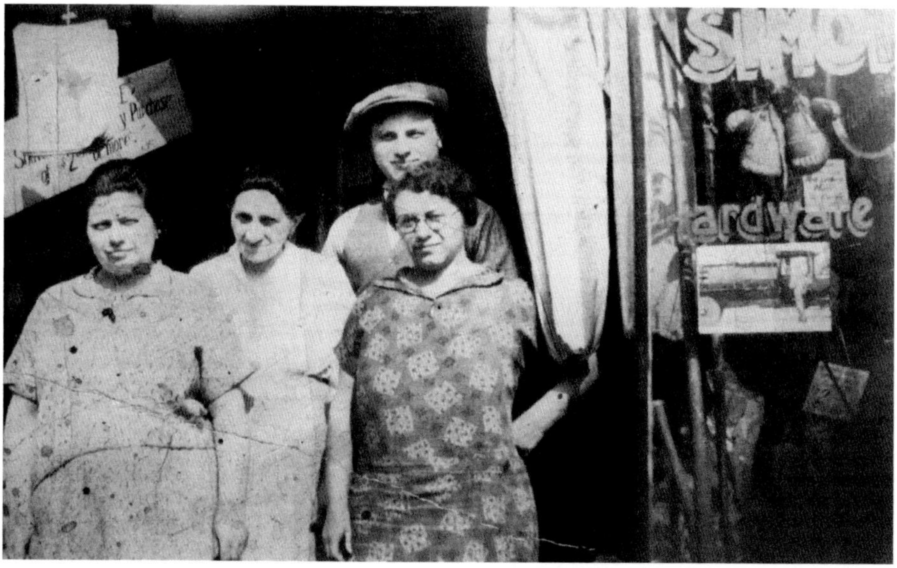

Founded by its namesake in 1887, Simon Harris Sporting Goods was a Baltimore institution for over one hundred years, remembered for its motto "Your Old Friend Simon Harris." Customers recall stacks of sporting goods from boxing gloves to gym shoes jumbled together and piled high. Here Yetta Harris and her children Jennie, Fannie and Samuel stand outside the storefront on the 200 block of Gay Street, circa 1924. *Gift of Selma Harris, 1986.83.3*

We used to eat lunch at Elsie Marvel's. She was basically a caterer, but she always kept a few tables going. Sometimes we ate at Lissy's deli, next to the market. Mayor McKeldin used to have lunch with my father occasionally, but they would drive over to Sussman and Lev on Baltimore Street or to Attman's on Lombard. The street always seemed to be busy, crowded, noisy. People and cars and the No. 15 streetcar rumbling through. Many would shop in the Belair Market, patronizing Helfenbein, Herling, Muscolino, Lapaglia, Raffo, Geppi.

The Jewish family-owned Gay Street stores were never seen to be in direct competition with the Jewish family-owned stores at Howard and Lexington Streets. They made no claim to offer fashion or prestigious brand names; they opted instead to offer lower prices and easy credit. It seemed to work. But by the 1960s, the glory days of the Jewish retailers' life on Gay Street had come and gone. The great names that once defined the time and the place were no more. Gay Street, as a Jewish-dominated shopping neighborhood, is now a story in collective memory, along with Howard and Lexington, East Monument Street and Pimlico.

Originally published as "Gay Street," February 23, 2001.

Living "Over the Store"

Many a suburbanite in Jewish Baltimore, sitting poolside on a patio with a view of lush gardens, may have only a vague remembrance that his or her grandparents grew up sitting at a kitchen table—on the second floor of a row house with a view of the street. The first floor was the store, which provided the family's livelihood; the second is where the family lived, and up through World War II, " living over the store" defined life for many families in Jewish Baltimore. As those who lived the life recall it, work on the first floor and life on the second were fused.

In Highlandtown, Jerry Wilen lived over the family store, at 3814 Eastern Avenue, in the 1920s and into the 1930s. He recalls that all along Eastern Avenue were Jewish merchants whose families lived over their stores: at 3308, Reuben Grodnitsky, window shades; 3310, Paul's Jewelry; 3311, Schwartzman's, ladies' clothing; 3241, Blank's dry goods; 3304, Harry Isaacson's, ladies' clothing; 3318, Morris Snyder, men's clothing; 3319, Rose Caplan's shoes; 3323, Julius Farbman's five-and-ten.

But Leon Albin, a former member of the Maryland House of Delegates and now active in commercial real estate, makes the argument that no neighborhood had as many "over the store" residences as his old neighborhood:

> *Pennsylvania Avenue was the core of the lower section of West Baltimore, and together with the side streets, including Lanvale, Mosher and Pine Streets, and Myrtle and Lafayette Avenues, made up a solid neighborhood.*

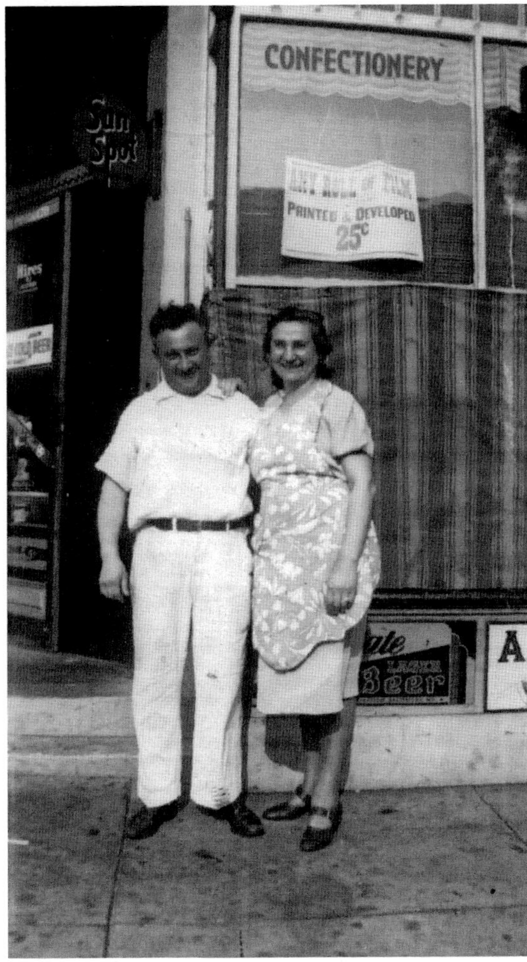

Jack and Pearl Raynor stand outside of their Waverly neighborhood confectionery shop in 1940. They opened the shop in 1938 and, after World War II, converted it to a liquor store. *Gift of Rita Malin, CP 24.2008.1.*

> *In it, many Jewish families were operating some sort of small business, with living quarters over the store.*
>
> *I lived at 912 Pennsylvania Avenue, where my father had a used clothing store, and our family of seven—my father, my mother and five of us children—lived over it. The bathtub was in one of the bedrooms and the toilet was in the hall. We kids grew up working in the family store. It was impossible to separate family life from business life.*

Near the Albin family on Pennsylvania Avenue lived the Amernicks, at 921, on the second floor over their men's clothing store; at 927, the Deitches, over their shoe store; and at 1347, the Hirshfelds, over their candy and tobacco store. Along Fremont Avenue, living on the second floor over their stores were the Baitches, the Weiners and the Gersteins; on Pine Street, the Bersonskys; and on Myrtle Avenue, the Dubanskys.

Former lieutenant governor Melvin "Mickey" Steinberg was born in 1933 at Franklin Square Hospital in West Baltimore, a few blocks from where his parents and he and his brother lived at 1723 West Lanvale Street—on the second floor, over his father's grocery store:

> *Throughout the area, there were Jewish families living on the second floor, and sometimes the third, because of sheer economics. It simply was not economically feasible for those small businesses to own or even rent two properties—one a home and the other a store. So they combined the store with the home.*
>
> *Then there was the convenience of living where you worked—my father opened the store at six in the morning and closed at eight at night, or later. If the store had been at another location, "travel time" would have meant losing hours off of the selling day in the morning and in the evening, and would impose a tremendous physical burden at the same time.*
>
> *It was the only life we knew. We kids would come home from school and usually get into the living areas of our homes by going through the store. It was the same throughout the neighborhood—down at the corner the Pinksys lived over their grocery store. Up the street, the Browns lived over their confectionery store. Across the street, the Barshefskys lived over their tailor shop. And you can be sure, in each of them, though life went on upstairs on the second floor, or behind the store, there was always somebody from the family in the store.*

Notwithstanding the ongoing commerce generated in the neighborhood by so many storefront businesses, there was a sense among the resident business families that theirs was a neighborhood—bound together by a commonality of lifestyle and an embrace of the institutions that provided a support system. As Leon Albin recalled:

> *The YM and YWHA was six blocks away. We played softball at PS 129, and my gang went often over the few blocks to Pennsylvania Avenue to the Royal Theater to see Cab Calloway and Louis Armstrong. Lexington Market was only about a mile away. Some of us became Bar Mitzvah at the Franklin Street shul near Fremont, Ohr Knesset Israel-Anshe Sphard, and some went to the Talmud Torah on West Lexington Street. With so much going on in our neighborhood, we considered ourselves lucky.*

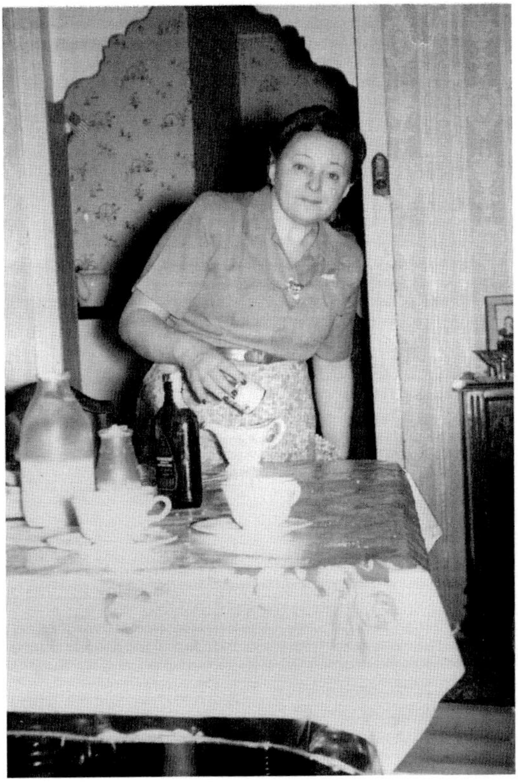

Rose Livov in her dining room, late 1930s. Rose and her husband, Reuben, lived above Livov Brothers Furriers, which Reuben owned with his brother David, on East Baltimore Street. Livov Brothers Furriers was also known as the Livov Brothers Ladies Model Shop. *Courtesy of Norma Wolod, L2006.20.10.*

Jonas Yousem was born at 1801 West Lafayette Avenue in 1933 and grew up in the same West Baltimore neighborhood as Mickey Steinberg, Leon Albin and another friend, Jerry Leiber, who lived with his family over their confectionery store at Riggs and McKean Avenues:

> *We were raised working in the store on the first floor and living in back of the store and on the second floor. We all worked in the store. When I was old enough to lift, I started bagging potatoes and sorting out soda bottles by brands to turn them in to the companies for cash. The neighborhood was full of Jewish-owned grocery stores. Spivak's was at Monroe and Lanvale Streets, Giller's at Mosher Street and Kirby Lane.*
>
> *Family life revolved around the family store. When we ate in our dining room in back of our store, my mother sat so she could see what was going on in the store. No matter what she was doing—cooking, eating or whatever—if she saw a customer, she would leave the kitchen or dining room and go into the store to wait on the customer.*

We had our own playground—the alleys behind the stores. Boys played stickball and "Red Rover," the girls hopscotch and jump rope. Vacations among those live-over-the store families were out of the question—the only vacation I ever had was a two-day trip to Atlantic City with my father, and only because my mother stayed home to tend the store. Saturdays, after all, were the biggest days.

Saturdays were so busy and so important to the family that my brothers and I were Bar Mitzvah on a Thursday—because my parents could not afford to give up a Saturday's business.

Over in Canton, Ray Klein lived over the family store, Klein's Variety Store, at 3003 O'Donnell Street. He recalls that at 3001, the Selzer family had a shoe store and lived above it. Frieda Fritzie Pozanek recalls that her family had first a grocery store and then a restaurant and bar on the corner of Eastern Avenue and Eaton Street. "My husband's family lived over the store and I lived with them when I was first married," she says.

And in Towson, the Finkelstein family lived in back of and over their store. Jack Finkelstein recalls, "The living room and dining room were in back of the store; the bedrooms were on the third floor. In that dining room in back of the store is where we had *Shabbos* dinner every Friday night, and of course, all of our seders."

For these families, there was an ever-present sense that the store below was the well-spring of family life, that it forever needed tending, minding, worrying about. But the generation of Jewish Baltimoreans who lived and worked "over the store" has passed on. "Did we, as a Jewish family, miss living in houses that did not have a store on the first floor?" asks Leon Albin. "How could we? We didn't know any."

Originally published as "We Considered Ourselves Lucky," August 27, 2004.

When Doctors Made House Calls

From the 1920s through the 1960s, Northwest Baltimore was, by any measure, an East European village transplanted. The community functioned with a kind of stubborn insularity: it had its own stores, Hebrew schools, kosher butchers, synagogues and pharmacies. It also had its own coterie of doctors. All were Jewish and concentrated their practices in Northwest Baltimore—and they all made house calls.

One busy doctor in those days, serving Jewish patients between Park Circle and Belvedere Avenue, was Dr. Samuel V. Tompakov. Dr. Tompakov practiced in the Jewish community from 1945 to 1992. He remembers the days:

> *My office was at 3431 Park Heights Avenue, across from Sussman's drugstore. As did my colleagues, I started the day with office hours from 7:30 in the morning until about one o'clock—and then I started my house and hospital calls. I made as many as ten and twelve in a day. I opened my office again after dinner at around seven and then around ten made additional house calls through the evening, sometimes as late as one o'clock in the morning.*
>
> *Often, in the dead of winter, I had to put on snow tires and trudge through the snow and ice. Then, typical of our practices, I would go home to sleep, be awakened at three in the morning with an emergency that required another house call. Sometimes there would be a second and third house call to make that same night and morning, and I would not get to bed at all. During the flu epidemic of the 1950s, I made as many as eighteen and twenty house calls a day. These days, the patient always goes to the*

> *doctor or the emergency rooms. In my day, we brought the doctor and the hospital to the patient. Medical care was the doctor coming to your house, carrying his little black bag.*

And what was in that little black bag? Here is the "hospital" the doctor brought into your home: stethoscope, otoscope (to look into the ear), ophthalmoscope (to look into eyes), needle and thread to sew sutures, syringes, bandages, morphine tablets, percussion hammer and surgical clamps to stop bleeding.

> *I will never forget one house call. The patient had fallen against a radiator and gashed his forehead open, and he was bleeding heavily. I stopped the bleeding temporarily, and managed to get him into my car. I took him to my office and stitched him up. But the most common calls were for acute respiratory problems, infectious diseases, heart attacks and high fevers.*

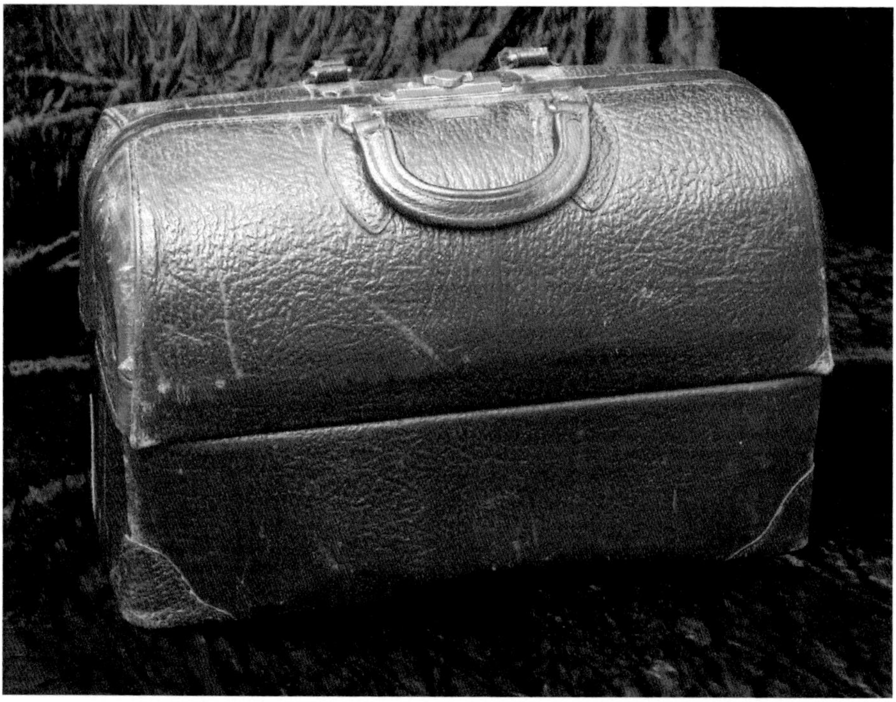

Medical bags like these were a familiar sight on the streets of Northwest Baltimore in the 1950s. *Gift in memory of Leonard J. Abramovitz, MD (son of Morris), and Jeanne D. Abramovitz by their children, 2001.26.149.*

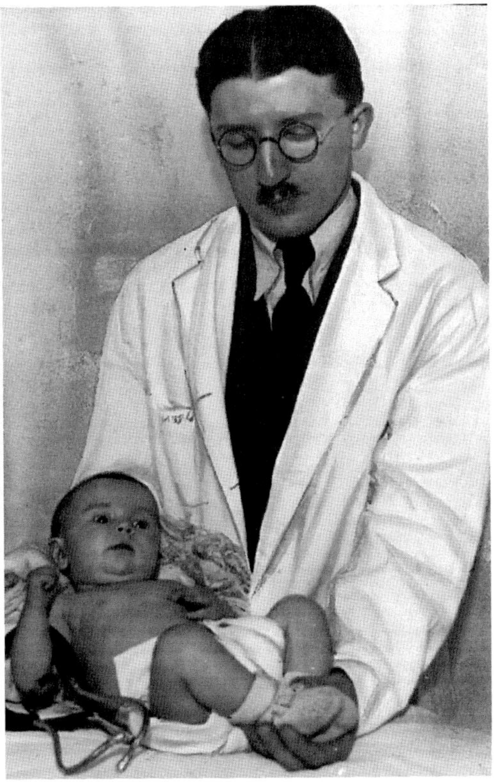

Dr. S. Shipley Glick working at the baby clinic, May 1930. *Courtesy of the University of Maryland Libraries, Special Collections and Hearst Corporation, CP 4.2012.7.*

Jewish doctors—general practitioners, pediatricians, even internists—who made house calls in the Park Heights corridor included Drs. S. Shipley Glick, Lester Coleman, Irvin Sauber, Leon Donner, Joseph Gross, Nathan Needle, A.L. Hornstein, Henry Seidel, Lester Caplan, Jerome Fineman and John Askin.

"By the way," Dr. Tompakov recalled, "the fee for house calls in 1945 was three dollars. I kept a little record book, and I remember that some people would pay one dollar and sometimes two dollars up front, and the rest they would pay later—sometimes."

Dr. S. Shipley Glick, whose offices were housed on the first floor of a row house at 4006 Park Heights Avenue (and who was honored by the University of Maryland at age ninety-three), recalled that in the 1950s, he was making as many as ten house calls every weekday and some on Saturdays and Sundays, too.

Dr. Glick made one of his most memorable house calls on the morning of July 22, 1929. He had taken a phone call from a worried parent, Evelyn McGruder. Mrs. McGruder's thirteen-year-old daughter, Ruth, was sitting in a treehouse in the back of their home at 5704 Ethelbert Avenue in Pimlico. Ruth was just recovering from scarlet fever, her mother said, and there she was sitting up in a tree. Could Dr Glick come at once?

Dr. Glick soon learned that the situation was more complicated than it sounded. At the time, a flagpole-sitting fad was sweeping over Baltimore. No one really sat on a flagpole. Instead, a kid would climb to the top of a tree, fashion a seat and perch there, determined to sit up in a tree longer than any other kid on the block. Ruth McGruder was one of the more determined kids.

Recalled Dr. Glick, "I arrived at the house and found that someone had placed a ladder for me to climb up to where Ruth was sitting. I examined her, balancing myself on the ladder. She was in excellent health. I tried to talk her into coming down, but she wouldn't hear of it. Of course, she eventually did—ten days later. But a kid from Highlandtown took the contest and set the record—fifty-five days."

All the doctors agree that they stopped making house calls in the Jewish community (and everywhere else) sometime in the early 1970s. The practice came to an end for a variety of reasons. First, the sophisticated technology for diagnosing and treatment could not be carried from place to place. Second, as the Jewish community moved farther and farther out, distances between office and homes became greater and too daunting and time-consuming to travel. "But there was something very special about those doctors' personal visits to the home," said Dr. Glick. "Today, patients and some quite sick people sit in doctors' waiting rooms and fill out insurance forms."

Anthony "Tony" Perlman started his practice in Baltimore in 1954 and retired a few years ago:

> *I have been led to believe by colleagues in other cities that house calls were very much a part of the culture of Jewish Baltimore. They would tell me that the number of house calls they made were nowhere as many in number as the Jewish doctors here in Baltimore made. You learned a great deal about your patients by visiting their homes. Times change. Today, a doctor might take care of a patient for twenty years and never have the opportunity of making a house call and seeing the patient in his own home surroundings.*

For all of the nostalgia for the doctor making his house call on you, there is general agreement that medical care—notwithstanding its sometimes off-putting complexity—is infinitely better than it used to be. But if you are one who still has a memory of the neighborhood doctor coming to your house with his little black satchel, with his fondly remembered personal, one-on-one touch, you may have trouble believing that.

Originally published as "Playing Doctor," February 2, 2001.

Last of a Breed: Installment Men of East Baltimore

As Jewish Baltimore grew in size and presence, certain businesses, lending themselves to the Jewish immigrants' needs and skills, came to be dominated by Jewish ownership. One was the scrap business; a second, the garment industry. There is a third, lesser known and less visible: what men in it called "the installment business." They are the heirs of a centuries-old tradition deeply rooted in Jewish life.

Here in Baltimore, Moses Hutzler started his department store empire as a peddler; Louis Blaustein (who founded American Oil), sold kerosene oil door-to-door in East Baltimore; and Isaac Hamburger sold hats (that his wife made) off his horse-drawn wagon through the very same blocks. They were among a large group of Jewish immigrants who found themselves with pushcarts and horse-drawn wagons buying pots and pans and sheets and towels from Jacob Epstein's Bargain House and selling the merchandise door-to-door all over the city, the state and beyond. Substitute automobiles for horses and wagons, and the Hanover Street wholesale houses for the Baltimore Bargain House, and you have the modern-day peddlers, a generation of "installment men" who flourished in Baltimore into the 1980s.

According to Hilford Caplan, who was in the business thirty years, it was a simple matter of selling merchandise door-to-door on the "installment plan"; that is, "a minimum amount of cash down, the remainder to be paid out in small installments over time. They sold umbrellas, women's dresses, men's suits, furniture, appliances—often strapping a TV set to the roof of the car."

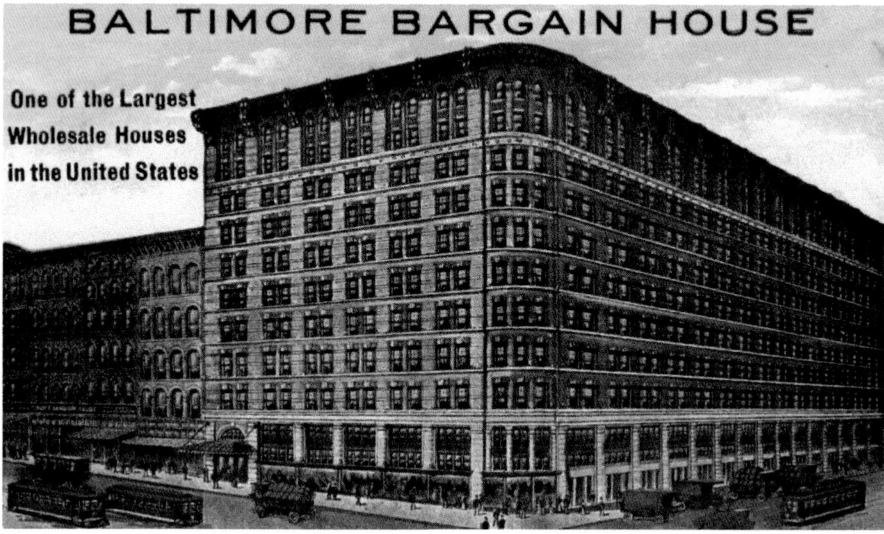

The Baltimore Bargain House, opened by Jacob Epstein in 1881, was a major source of wholesale goods for the Jewish peddlers of Baltimore into the 1920s. Postcard, Baltimore Bargain House, circa 1915. *1989.69.1.*

The wholesale houses of Hopkins Place and South Hanover Streets were their warehouses, the row house streets of East Baltimore were their marketplaces and their unofficial "offices" were the nearby delis.

Stanley "Rocky" Rutkovitz knew the life:

> *I would start out in the morning, with a trunk full of samples—clothing, radios, small appliances and head for East Baltimore—Caroline, Wolfe, and Eden Streets, Central Avenue and Broadway. I'd call on my customers to collect money owed and to sell new merchandise at the same time. Most mornings I would drive first to one of the wholesale houses downtown to pick up merchandise. Sometimes, in the case where we would be selling a living room suite, I would drive my customer over to one of the wholesale warehouses catering to installment houses—White and Herman comes to mind.*
>
> *Making my stops in East Baltimore, I would often run into my competitors. Alvin Fisher, Hilford Caplan, Marvin Schwartz, the guys working for the stores from Al Fradkin, Massey, Kovens, Checket, Charles Fish, Goldschmidt, Elgin Furniture Company, Berlin and Lewis. I'd learn which wholesaler was offering attractive buys, which customers were to be avoided.*
>
> *Sometime around lunchtime I would head for S&H deli, or, depending on the year, Belman's at Baltimore and Ann Streets, or Attman's, or Jack's*

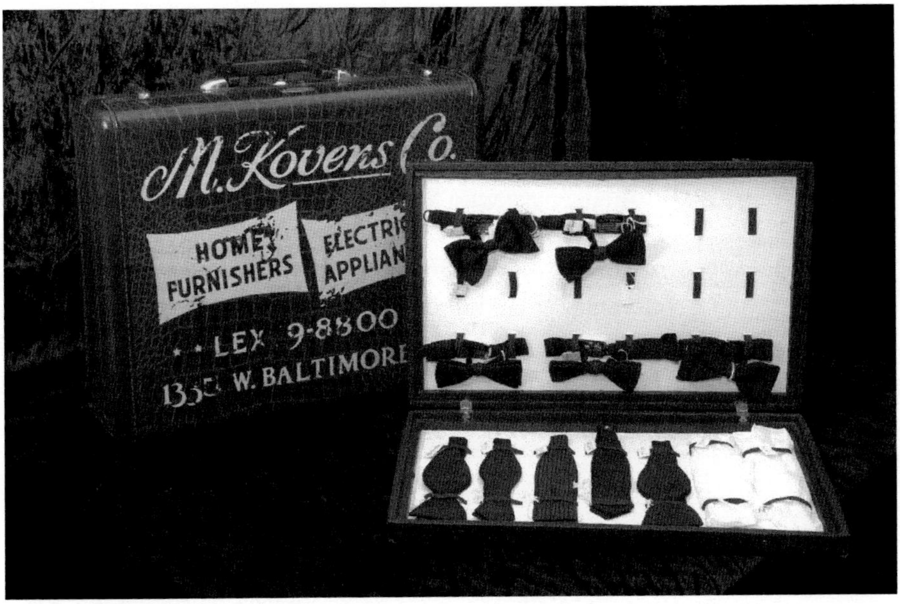

Saleman's kits, like these for Resisto Ties and Kovens Furniture, accompanied Baltimore's mid-century peddlers all around town. *Museum purchase and gift of Abe and Faye (Kovens) Adler, 1996.64.19 and 2001.63.1.*

> *on Lombard Street. Here I knew I could not only eat a great deli lunch, Jewish-style, but wash up, make a few phone calls, meet the guys in the same line of work and share ideas.*

S&H was in fact a family business, the families of Syd Cohen and his wife, Gerry, and Henry Cohen and his wife, Doris. They were the children of Harry and Sarah Kaplonsky Cohen. Doris Cohen remembers: "It was like one big family. Henry was the cashier, Sarah was in the kitchen; she made all of our soups and gefilte fish herself. Everybody ate the same thing, everybody was in business, and everybody was Jewish— regulars like Sam Feigan, Herbie Block, Herbie Henderson, Joe Bloom. The big seller was our hot roast beef sandwich smothered in gravy."

Ms. Cohen talks of some of the installment men who seemed to have all the time in the world for lunch. "They ate, lingered and played the pinball machines and sometimes kept a card game going."

This is the S&H deli that traces its origins to founder Harry E. Cohen, who came to Baltimore in 1906 at age sixteen with his brother, Sam. In 1913, he married Sarah Kaplonsky, and by 1919, the Cohens had scraped together enough money to buy a little delicatessen at 1427 East Baltimore Street. Harry ran the cash register and the restaurant operation and became famous in the neighborhood for his noodle kugel, potato latkes, knishes, sauerkraut and pickled onions, cucumbers and green tomatoes. It would be Harry's sons and their wives who would be the hosts in the succeeding era when the S&H business changed—from serving families living in the neighborhood to installment men selling in the neighborhood.

Mr. Rutkovitz recalls going back to work after lunch: "In the afternoons we'd do pretty much the same thing we did in the morning, driving back and forth between customers and wholesalers and back to customers. We were usually able to get home by dinnertime. Except for Friday night. Many of our customers got paid on Fridays, so we would be out on the street, summer and winter, in heat and cold, in the light and in the dark, until ten o'clock."

Why did the business mushroom so after the war? Caplan says:

> *There were a lot of men coming back after the war, looking for opportunity. The installment business beckoned. It was easy to get into. It required no special education. You needed no inventory, very little cash. All it took was hard work, and the get-up-and-go to knock on doors and drive all over the place. And it was, up until more recent years, comfortable and safe. We would build up special and warm relationships with our customers.*

Alvin Fisher was typical of the young men who went into the business after World War II. In 1946, in his early twenties, out of the army and with little capital and no special skills, he was looking to find his way in the postwar world. He reunited with an old friend, Harry Weitzman, then working for Leon Levi, the mammoth jewelry and appliance store at Eutaw and Lexington Streets. The two old friends became partners, and together, in the blocks encircling Johns Hopkins Hospital, they knocked on doors. "There were hundreds of us out there on those streets. We bought and sold pillowcases and sheets and bedspreads from Standard Textiles, watches from Baltimore Jewelry Company, raincoats from Baltimore Raincoat Company. For most of us, for all of the hard work and the long hours, I think the business treated us well."

But beginning sometime in the late 1970s, the market for the installment salesmen diminished and ultimately all but disappeared, as did most of the delis that catered to them. Epochal changes in the marketplace—social, economic and political—so reduced demand that the business lost its viability. The installment men depended on the delis, and the delis depended on the installment men; when they could no longer depend on each other, the relationship dissolved.

This generation of Jewish peddlers in Baltimore is the last in a long line, some of whom built many of Baltimore's giant wholesale and retailing businesses, beginning with the first waves of immigrants arriving in Baltimore in the 1850s. The life they led, and the role they played in the history of Jewish Baltimore, lives now only in the stories they tell about it.

Originally published as "Last of a Breed," July 27, 2001.

PART 4

Recreation and Leisure

Recalling Jewish life in earlier decades, Baltimore Jews remember the aromas of traditional food, the excitement of ball games and amusement parks and the sometimes-painful experience of adolescence. In these stories of recreation and leisure, as one might expect, the pleasures of life predominate.

For many, memories of youthful amusement are suffused with nostalgia, when the world—and their lives—lay before them, and the compromises of old age were still far removed. So, these elegies to the past are partly about innocence, partly about experience, and always about the passage of time in the course of individual lives.

Romancing the Coddie

Why is the Baltimore Jewish community different from all other Jewish communities? There is one certain answer: the coddie. The coddie was born in Baltimore and is offered and consumed only in Baltimore, and you will not find it in any other Jewish community on earth.

For those of you who do not know what a coddie is—you are from out of town, you are young or you have been living in a cave—a coddie looks like a codfish cake, tastes like a codfish cake. Only it isn't. Coddies (with crackers and mustard) have been sold in most of the delis in Baltimore since 1910.

The coddie's origins are vague, but the way the descendants of the Louis Cohen family tell the story, it was grandfather Louis Cohen's wife, Fannie Jacobson Cohen, who created the coddie as we know it. According to Mrs. Elaine Cohen Alpert, granddaughter of Louis Cohen, "In 1910, my grandparents were living at 131 South Bond Street. They eked out a living with their small confectionery stand in the Belair Market. They sold sodas and cookies, candies, potato chips, sandwiches. They were searching for something new, something no one else would have."

Fannie Cohen was the cook. Mrs. Alpert says she always understood that on a day in 1910, grandmother Fannie was mashing potatoes and making french fries and got the idea of taking a handful of potato—formed larger than a codfish ball, smaller than a codfish cake—and deep-frying it to see what it tasted like. She decided it needed something, and nearby was a container of codfish flakes, used in those days for flavoring. As this version of the story goes, Mrs. Cohen thought to sprinkle codfish flakes on the potato cake and then to deep-fry it. She applied salt and pepper and decided it would do.

She took a batch of the fried potato cakes to the stall in the Belair Market, and for some reason, Mr. Cohen put the cakes between two crackers. Tradition has it that a customer asked for the mustard. And there it was, Baltimore's (and the world's) first coddie—deep-fried codfish-flavored potato between two saltines, floating in mustard. It was the first coddie in the history of the world.

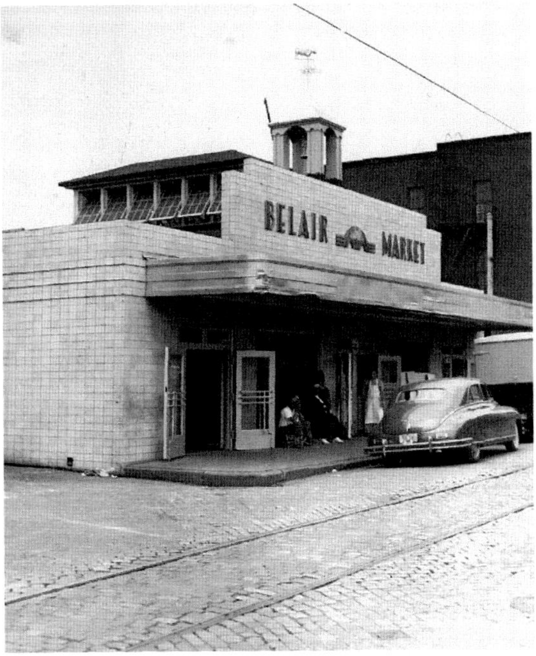

The Cohen family maintains that their ice cream stall, once located at the Belair Market, offered Baltimore's first taste of the iconic coddie. Belair Market, circa 1950. *Courtesy of the University of Maryland Libraries, Special Collections and Hearst Corporation, CP 4.2012.6.*

But of course the history of the coddie is more complicated. An 1889 Jewish cookbook gives a recipe for codfish balls that is almost word-for-word the recipe for the present-day coddie:

> *Put the fish to soak overnight in lukewarm water. Change again in the morning and wash off all the salt. Cut into pieces and boil about fifteen minutes. Pour off this water and put on to boil again with boiling water. Boil twenty minutes. Drain off water, put on platter to cool and pick to pieces as fine as possible, removing skin and bone. Add an equal quantity of mashed potatoes, a lump of butter, salt and pepper. Beat up an egg and work into dough. Flour hands and form. Fry in hot butter or drippings.*

That is an 1889 recipe for a modern-day coddie—fish-flavored potato, deep-fried, salted and peppered.

So in 1910, did Mrs. Cohen know about the codfish ball? Even if she did, she nonetheless can take credit for giving it a new shape and serving it on crackers with mustard.

But back to the Cohens in the early 1900s in the Belair Market. By now, word was out along Gay Street about Mr. Cohen's codfish cakes, which became shortened to "coddies." In no time at all, with the help of son Harry (who started working in the business when he was twelve), from the 1920s through the 1970s, Cohen's Coddies trucks were delivering coddies to delis all over town. So successful were Cohen's coddies that Mr. Cohen himself was moved to record the success for history.

On the back of a sales slip showing the address of Cohen's modest manufacturing plant (Mrs. Alpert says it was a garage) at 215–217 Bethel Street, he wrote for posterity: "Sixty years ago on April 20, 1910, L. Cohen of Old Town made and sold the first coddie (codfish cake) to the folks that came to his little soda water and ice cream stand in the Blear [*sic*] Market. They were so delicious and appetizing that people from all over came to his stand to eat and enjoy them with his delicious chocolate sodas. Today in over five hundred stores in Baltimore you buy the same coddie."

Mr. Cohen wrote that in 1970. But since then, others have had a go at making coddies, and although you can still buy coddies (same crackers, same mustard and very good indeed), they are not the original Cohen's Coddies. Cohen made his last coddie in 1971.

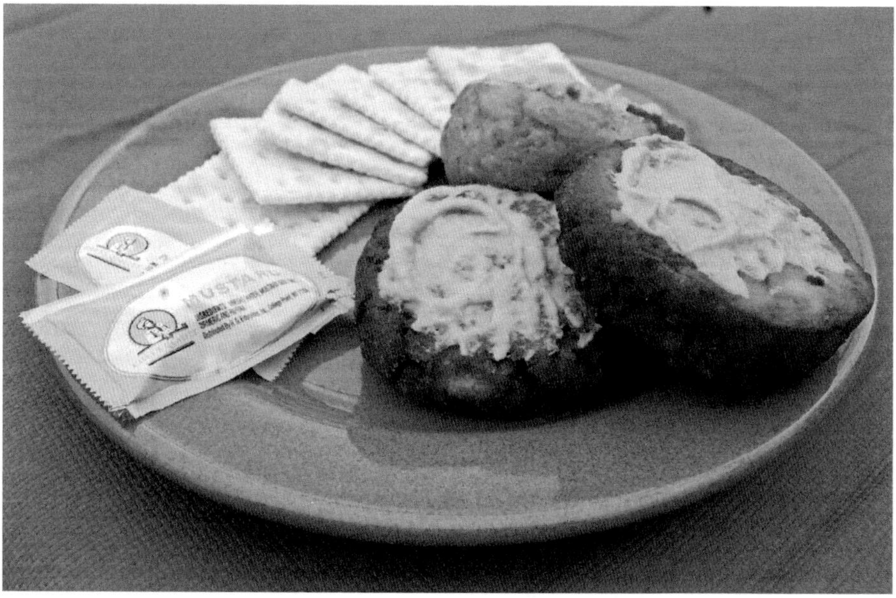

While recipes may differ slightly, at least one thing remains the same: the only way to eat a coddie is with yellow mustard! *Photograph by Elena Rosemond-Hoerr.*

Some years ago, Seymour Attman, the late, lamented owner and operator of Attman's on East Lombard Street, said he sold as many as two hundred coddies on an ordinary day:

> *On a day where there are parties, like the Sunday afternoon of a football game, we can sell a thousand in a morning. In whatever deli coddies are sold today, it's the deli that is making them. Nobody is making them and distributing them, like Cohen did in the old days. Those days died with Louis Cohen and Cohen's Famous Coddies. How do I make my coddies? I don't give out my exact recipes, but we take potato, mix in cracker meal, sprinkle it with a fish-flavored powder, deep fry it, add seasoning—Old Bay and salt and pepper—and then pour in a bit of vegetable oil.*

David Hess, a manager at Suburban House on Reisterstown Road, tells a similar story, and he uses a similar but not identical recipe: "We put ground-up fish in our coddies. Any kind of fish, not just codfish. To get that fish flavor. We sell at least one hundred coddies a day, on a slow day. We can double that on a busy day. For Super Bowl parties, we sell a couple of thousand coddies." Brian Snyder, manager at Snyder's Deli in the Pink Mall, also sells fifty to one hundred coddies a day. "For the fish flavor," he says, "we use a fish paste."

What is it about deep-fried potato, seasoning, a hint of fish flavor (sometimes real, sometimes artificial) between crackers and swimming in mustard that drives Baltimore Jews crazy? And why is the coddie to be had only in Baltimore? It has to do with memory, of growing up in the old neighborhood, of friends you knew in elementary school, of corner confectionery stores and of the mystic power of "a coddie and chocolate soda" to send the film of the mind reeling backward, into the long-ago world of Jewish Baltimore.

Originally published as "In the Cods," June 22, 2001.

Getting Schmaltzy: Jewish Baltimore's Restaurant Row

It was a way of life. On Sunday evenings in the 1930s and 1940s, the sidewalks along both sides of the 800, 900 and 1000 blocks of East Baltimore Street were crowded with families going into and coming out of the restaurants that made up Jewish Baltimore's first, last and only "Restaurant Row." They are all gone, taking with them the memory of the largest concentration of Jewish foods south of New York, including but not limited to: corned beef, *kishka*, chopped liver, *latkes*, gefilte fish, roast chicken, *helzel*, brisket, *pirogen*, matzoh ball soup, *schav* and *tsimmes*.

Miriam Waitsman, whose family at different times owned both the Vienna and Silverman's, recalled, "Oscar Shulman, who owned Shulman's Roumanian Restaurant [1033 East Baltimore Street], served a huge steak on a wooden plank. The plank had a groove that ran around the edge, and the juices from the steak would run off into this groove. It was at least two and a half pounds. But I doubt they weighed it."

Sussman and Lev at 923 East Baltimore was the first full-scale delicatessen-restaurant in Baltimore. The number and variety of its sandwiches were legendary. Marty Lev, son of the owner/operating family, recalled, "An early menu offered lox and cream cheese, spiced beef, roast beef, corned beef, salami and chopped liver and an invitation to wash it all down with an Almond Smash."

The Vienna was at 810 East Baltimore Street. Selma Silverman Pressman, whose father and mother, Isadore and Tillie, owned and operated the Vienna, recalled:

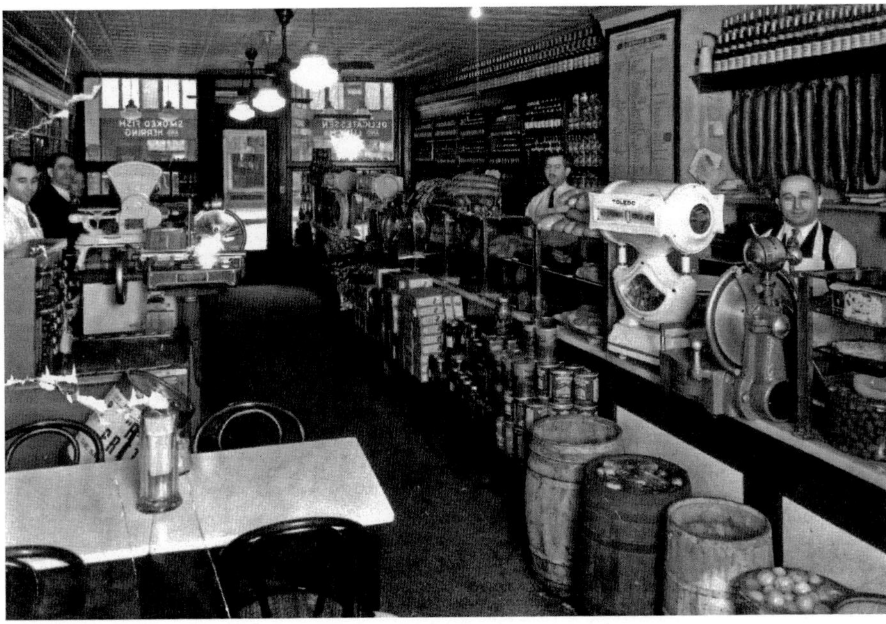

The clerks of the Sussman and Lev Delicatessen pose for a photograph in the first full-scale delicatessen-restaurant in Baltimore, located at 923 East Baltimore Street. *Gift of Martin Lev, 1991.140.2.*

> *So many families came in at one time on Sunday nights that sometimes the help couldn't handle it all or wouldn't. So we children, and there were five of us, did. We did everything. Help in the kitchen. Wait tables. Clean up. The Vienna offered the usual Jewish fare—brisket and gefilte fish were the favorites. But on our printed menu we featured Stuffed Vienna Kishke, meat blintzes and pickled herring. But I thought our desserts were among the best along East Baltimore Street. My mother made them all. Fruit tarts, jelly tarts, apple pie—and the strudel! Fantastic strudel! Apple and apricot, poppy seed and cherry and peach!*

Silverman's Dairy restaurant was at 1008 East Baltimore Street. Miriam Waitsman, who grew up over the store, recalls, "Silverman's was strictly dairy. We served no meat. Our menu offered lots of *kreplach* and cheese and fruit *blintzes*. Fish was very popular—baked and fried. Dairy restaurants were very popular in those days because many patrons, all immigrant Jews, were often wary of eating meat outside of their homes. They were worried that it might not meet their own standards of *kashrut*."

Of the New York Dairy at 827 East Baltimore, some held that you could get a heart attack just by looking at the menu. It offered five

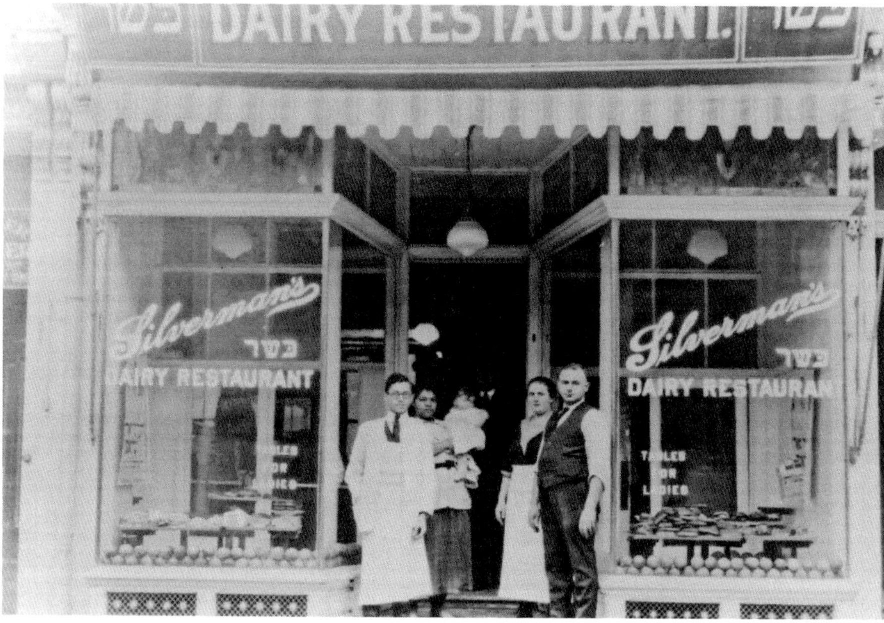

Tillie and Isadore Silverman stand outside one of their two Baltimore restaurants, Silverman's Dairy Restaurant, located on East Baltimore Street, with counterman Harry Greenspan and an unnamed housekeeper. *Gift of Miriam Waitsman, 1990.84.2a.*

kinds of herring—schmaltz, chopped and pickled and fried and tomato herring—imported and domestic. For soups, you could choose from cabbage, potato, borscht (hot and cold, with or without sour cream), *schav* and sour cream, rice and milk, noodles and milk.

Offered, too, were eleven different kinds of fish, including carp, rock, gefilte and white spots, boiled or baked. Also, cheese kreplach, potato and *kasha* pirogen, *schmetna* (vegetables with sour cream), strawberries and heavy cream, potato and cream, cheese and cream. A popular dessert was stewed prunes.

Ira Askin remembers going to Silverman's every Sunday for lunch. "My father would pick us up around noon at Chizuk Amuno, then on Eutaw Place, right after Hebrew school. I have a clear memory of those lunches. We always had the same waiter, Seth, who wore an alpaca jacket, stained with bits of the food he had been serving. We all started with soup. It was served hot in a pewter bowl, and then Seth would pour it into soup bowls. Borscht and matzoh ball soup were the favorites."

Al Kilberg was born and raised at 29 North Ann Street, near Fairmount Avenue. He recalled, "My father would take me to Shulman's. We always ordered the steak, and it came out sizzling on a wooden platter. My father was a member of Brith Shalom, and so often when we left Shulman's after dinner we would go to Brith Shalom Hall down the street, to see, maybe, a violin concert."

These storied blocks, running from the Fallsway on the west to Central Avenue on the east, and taking in the blocks all the way at least to Patterson Park, made up not just Jewish Baltimore's gustatory center but its cultural center as well. It was to these blocks that, beginning in the 1880s, immigrants fleeing the pogroms of Eastern Europe made their way from the Locust Point piers. The disembarking Italians, Greeks, Poles and Slovaks found work and settled in and around the waterfront. But the Jews gravitated to these blocks of East Baltimore Street because the word was out to them that that's where the commerce was.

Obsessed with "making it in America" and imbued with the ancient Jewish sense of *tzedakah* (philanthropy), the immigrants came together and founded self-help organizations. Most were centered in this very same area. The Workmen's Circle headquarters was at 1029, and the *Jewish Daily Forward* newspaper was upstairs. Brith Shalom was at 1012, Henrietta Szold's night school was nearby and the JEA (Jewish Educational Alliance) was a few blocks away at Central. Nearby was the Hebrew Free Loan Society. And on Lloyd Street, which intersected Baltimore Street, were the Lloyd Street Synagogue and the Chizuk Amuno Synagogue (which became B'nai Israel).

There were lots of restaurants in Baltimore in those days, including some fondly remembered—Miller Brothers in the 100 block of East Fayette Street, Marconi's in the 300 block of West Saratoga Street and Jimmy Wu's in the 1900 block of North Charles Street. But for all their prominence, in none of them could you get a two-and-a-half-pound steak on a wooden plank, a dozen varieties of home-made strudel, oversized cheese blintzes, mile-high chopped liver sandwiches washed down with a bottle of Almond Smash or five different kinds of herring (imported and domestic). For these, the *haimish* food of your (or your parents' or grandparents') youth, you had to go to Jewish Baltimore's Restaurant Row, the 800, 900 and 1000 blocks of East Baltimore Street.

Originally published as "Getting Schmaltzy," August 25, 2006.

The Woodlands: Recreation for Baltimore's Jewish Poor

On the night of July 12, 1938, about thirty or so twelve-year-old boys and girls are sitting around a campfire. It is a starlit night, in a pastoral setting, far from the noise and the lights of the city. The children are chattering and giggling, as twelve-year-olds sitting around a campfire on a summer night will do. The talk is about the next day's swimming session set for the morning, the color war in the afternoon and the softball game after supper. You might think this is a scene from Camp Tapawingo in Maine, Owaissa in Massachusetts, Camp Cody in Pennsylvania or even Louise or Airy in Western Maryland.

But this summer camp is not like any summer camp you may know about. This is Camp Woodlands, in Catonsville in Baltimore County, hugging the western edge of Baltimore City. It is different because each of the campers sitting around the fire that night is in the class of the "underprivileged," here for a week, free—courtesy of the Associated Jewish Charities. (In 1950, when Ben Katzner was president of the Associated, he observed of the admissions, "A very few paid what they could.")

We welcome you to Camp Woodlands,
we're mighty glad you're here,
We'll have the place ring out the word,
with a mighty cheer…

Camp Woodlands was an outgrowth of, and a second life for, what was originally Woodlands Country Estates. The camp itself came into being

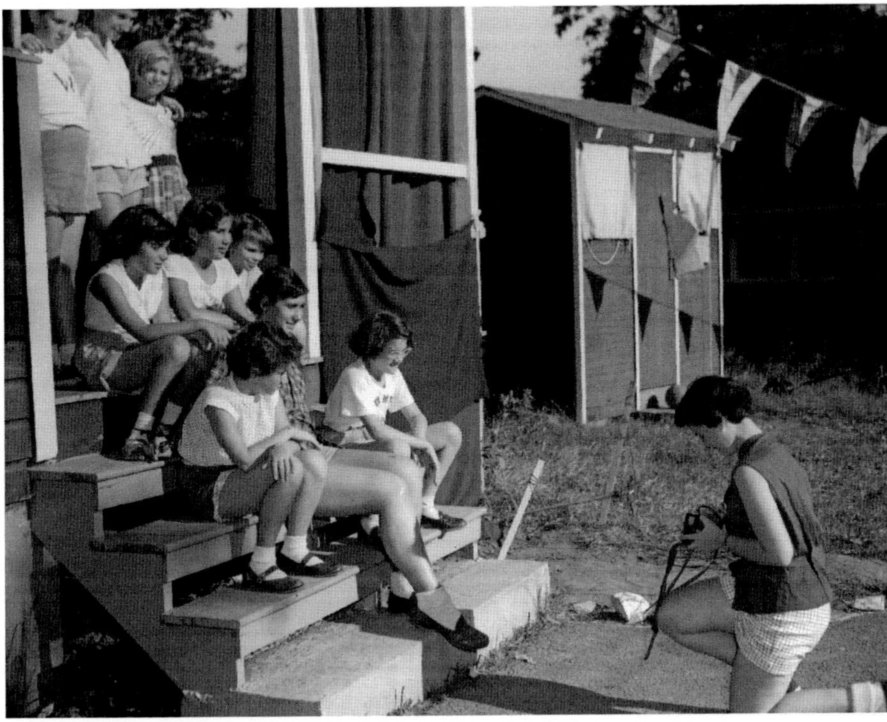

Campers pose on their bunk steps for a group photograph, August 1953. *Gift of the Jewish Community Center of Baltimore, 1995.98.125.*

because the Associated Jewish Charities recognized an unmet need among Jewish Baltimore's poor: respite in the country to escape Baltimore's mercilessly hot summers.

In no time, Jewish Social Services had all of the many rooms in Woodlands Estates mansion filled with Jewish families. Harry Greenstein, then representing Maryland's State Relief organization, said, "There were enough poor to go around. This is little enough to do to help make life bearable for those who have nothing above the bare margin of existence."

The records of the founding of Woodlands Country Estates are dominated by the names of the Jewish leadership of the 1920s and 1930s: Milton Westheimer (investment banker), Mrs. Walter Sondheim Sr. (Hochschild, Kohn department store), Jacob Blaustein (American Oil), Elkan Myers (D. Myers and Sons), Manuel Hendler (Hendler's ice cream), Isaac Hamburger (retail clothing store) and Milton Halle (shoe manufacturing).

In 1935, the facility was greatly expanded, with a new wing that included a recreation hall, a dining room and administrative offices. The expansion was made possible through two legacies—one given by David Myers (father of community leader Elkan Myers) and the estate of Mr. and Mrs. Julius Levy, long identified with the M.S. Levy Company, manufacturers of straw hats.

According to a report written by Miss Annette Alperin, a social worker, "In 1930 a vacation is an unheard of luxury for these poor families. In 1930, approximately 460 families were guests, 119 were mothers, four were fathers, 336 were children unaccompanied by a parent. We had more than 950 applications, so we had to turn down many." She said the meals were well balanced and nourishing and that the staff was providing excellent service to the guests. But she concluded that "more children need to be given the opportunity of enjoying a week or two in these wholesome surroundings." She recommended that Woodlands Country Estates be converted to a children's summer camp: "Converting the country home and estate into a camp for children would solve the problem. The consensus seems to be that this should be done."

So it was. In the late 1930s, and over a few years in transitioning, bunks and camp facilities for twelve-year-olds were built, and Woodlands Country Estates (for families) became Camp Woodlands (for children).

Nathan Cantor was a counselor in Camp Woodlands and recalls:

> *There were five bunkhouses in excellent condition, each slept sixteen kids and two counselors. There was a so-called Big House, which contained the dining hall and administrative office, and where the kids would put on shows. There was, too, a softball diamond, a basketball court and a campfire setting with benches all around.*
>
> *Swimming was another problem. We did not have a swimming pool or a lake on the grounds, but we were near a public pool in Catonsville, owned and operated by Baltimore County. Remember the times. Jews were not welcome in a Catonsville swimming pool and the sight of a busload of 50 Jewish kids coming into this neighborhood swimming pool, well, when we approached the pool director about the matter, he was, let's say, hesitant.*
>
> *He thought a bit and then said, "Tell you what. You bring the kids in before noon, any day. That's when the place is empty. That ought to work." For him, it did. Camp Woodlands kids got to swim in the Catonsville neighborhood swimming pool, and the Catonsville neighbors never had to face the problem of all the Jewish kids swimming in their neighborhood pool.*

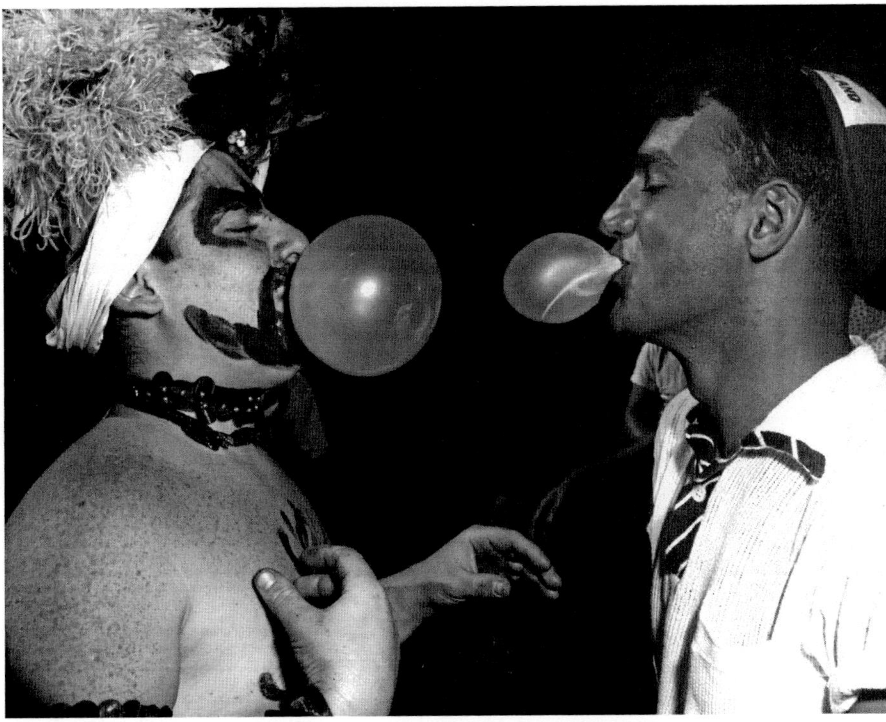

Swimming, sports and Sabbath services were all a part of Camp Woodlands life, but so was campfire fun. Here, camp staff put on some evening entertainment in August 1953. *Gift of the Jewish Community Center of Baltimore, 1995.98.131.*

We kept the camp "Jewish." We served kosher food, we had Friday night and Saturday morning services. Brief ones, yes, but we had them.

Camp Woodlands closed in the early 1950s to make way for the Baltimore Beltway. Motorists speeding west on the Baltimore Beltway pass Exit 12 uneventfully. They cannot know that within view, off to their right, there once stood the Big House of Woodlands Country Estates and the bunks and the playing fields of Camp Woodlands, which were buried beneath a complex of buildings known as the Western School of Technology. The plot is bounded on the north by Maiden Choice Lane, on the east by Kenwood Road and on the west by Paradise Avenue. With the Beltway running through it, it is hard to know the southern border of the property.

Nothing remains of the resort house and the summer camp—of the bunks, the Big House, the basketball court, the campfire circle, the singing of the children:

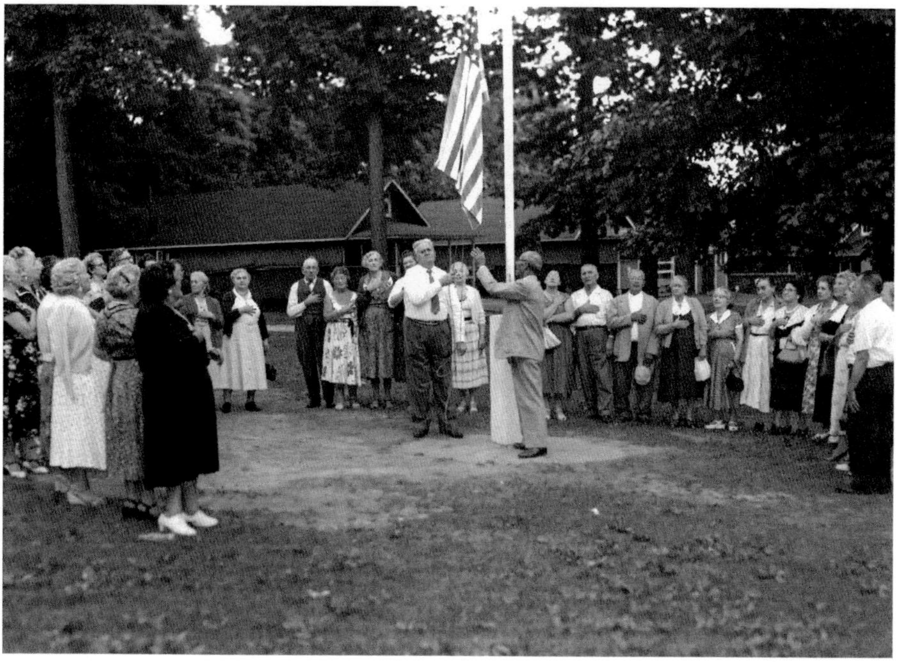

In what was possibly one of the last events held at Camp Woodlands before it was torn down to make way for the Beltway, "Golden Agers" reverently salute the American flag, hands over hearts, marking the end of the summer and the end of an era in August 1956. *Gift of the Jewish Community Center of Baltimore, 1995.98.47.*

We'll sing you in, we'll sing you out, for you we'll raise a mighty shout,
Hail, Hail, the gang's all here, Woodlands is what it's about.

Woodlands Country Estates is gone, and Camp Woodlands is gone. And that's what it's all about.

Originally published as "West of Paradise," November 24, 2006.

A League of Their Own: Talmud Torah Softball

It was, like, Goldberg-to-Cohen-to-Snyder—*Whoosh! Whoosh! Whoosh!* Double play! Don't laugh: the young twelve- and thirteen-year-old softball players pulling off this dazzling double play on a Sunday afternoon in 1936 were not just serious softball players. They were serious Hebrew school students—studying at one of the six Hebrew schools that made up the Talmud Torah softball league—Jewish Baltimore's first Hebrew school softball league.

The arrangement seems to have been the idea of the late Dr. Louis L. Kaplan, then-director of Jewish Education in Baltimore. According to his son-in-law, Efrem Potts, "He not only conceived the idea of softball teams as part of Jewish education, he often played on the faculty teams." Dr. Kaplan's daughter, Debbie Kaplan Potts, feels that her father was drawing on his fondness for stickball, from his days growing up in Brooklyn, New York. "He liked the idea of bringing together Talmud Torah boys from different parts of the city so they could get to know one another better. He urged students to play sports because he felt the change of pace and environment made them better students, and the competition made them better softball players—skills he thought useful in the world of twelve- and thirteen-year-old boys."

The Talmud Torahs served as Baltimore's first community-wide system committed to providing a Jewish education for Baltimore's Jewish children, in a time when synagogues for the most part did not provide it. That job had been left mainly to private tutors of varying abilities, education levels and standards. According to Harry London, a well-known educator in that system, "There was clearly a need for more order, structure and professionalism in teacher methods and curriculum and for planning, supervision and teacher

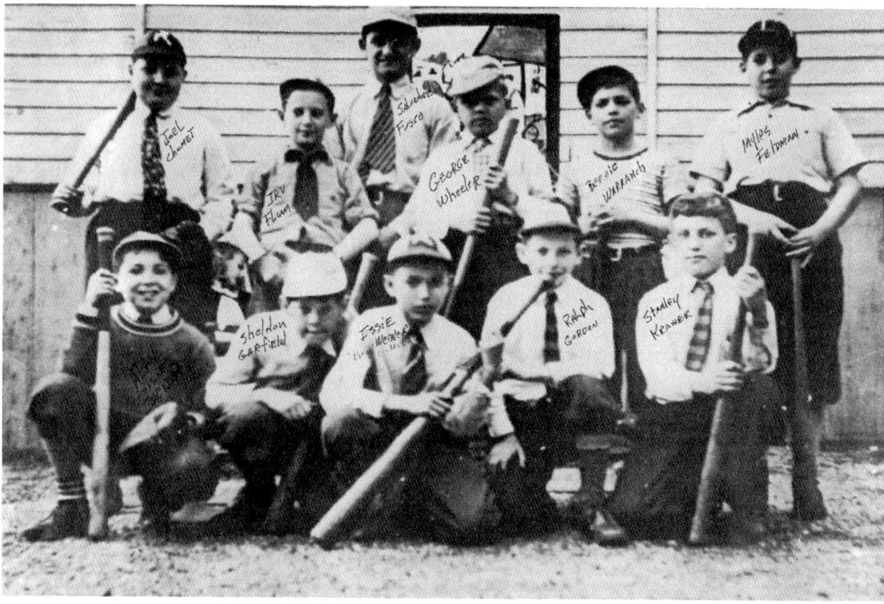

Those Hebrew schoolboys make quite the tough looking team! *Back row, left to right:* Joel Chomet, Irv Floam, Salvadore Fusco, George Wheeler, Bernie Warrauch and Myles Feldman; *front row, left to right:* Alan "Mike" Isekoff, Sheldon Garfield, "Boo" Goldstein, Ralph Gordon and Stanley Kramer. *Gift of Miriam Smelkinson, 1992.159.14.*

training. In addition, there was need for schools where girls could be more comfortably included. Enter the Talmud Torahs."

The first Talmud Torah opened in 1889. By the 1930s, there were six of them, and all were playing in the league: Baltimore Talmud Torah (22 North Broadway); Northwest (Callow Avenue and Lennox Street); Southwest (Eagle and Payson Streets); Western (743 West Lexington Street); South Baltimore (518 South Hanover Street); and Isaac Davidson (Shirley Avenue between Park Heights Avenue and Reisterstown Road).

Attendance in any of the Talmud Torahs was challenging academically. Mel Sykes recalls, "The curriculum was two hours a day, five days a week and included the Five Books of Moses, *siddur*, Joshua, Judges, Kings, laws, history, literature and Hebrew." Nonetheless, the students found time to field their own softball teams and to travel to and from the softball diamonds at Carroll Park, Patterson Park and the playground between Isaac Davidson Hebrew School and PS 59.

Dr. Barney Berman (Southwest) remembered, "About those softball games, I vividly remember the spirit and rivalry among those schools. Western Talmud

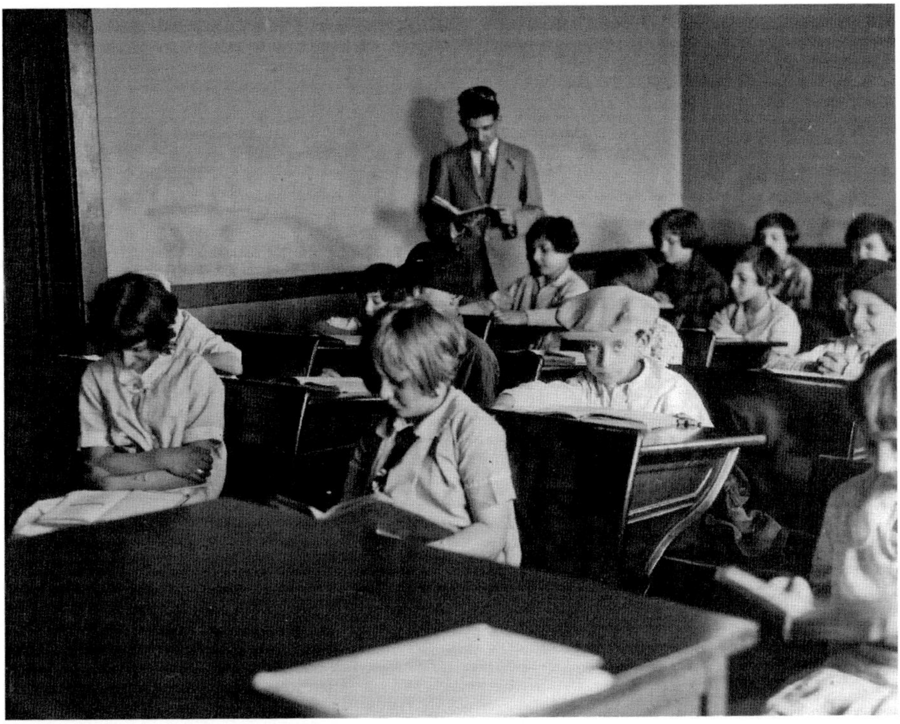

Hymen Saye teaching a coed class at Talmud Torah, 1928. *Gift of Hymen Saye, 1991.7.12.*

Torah and Baltimore Talmud Torah were seldom forces within the league. Year after year, the championship was bitterly contested by Simon Bugatch's Southwest Talmud Torah and the feared Sidney Esterson's Isaac Davidson."

Leonard Woolf (Isaac Davidson) recalled, "We used to travel to Patterson Park and Carroll Park for games with the other Talmud Torah schools. Once we were in Carroll Park to play Southwest Talmud Torah. And our coach saw that we were going to win. He said, 'Boys, these Southwest guys are tough losers. When you see the last out, pick up your glove and get the hell out.' We did, too."

But for the relatively few girls in the Talmud Torah, there was no softball. Muriel Woolf recalled, "It seemed to us girls that the boys were playing softball all of the time, and there wasn't much for us to do but sit on the sidelines and watch them. Which is what we did."

But the highlight of the league's year was the annual softball game between the all-star students (the best of the best from all of the schools' teams) and the teachers from all of the schools' faculties, at Gwynn Oak Park on the last Sunday afternoon in August. The Board of Jewish Education took over the park for the full day. Dr. Leonard Golombek (Southwest) remembers, "Streetcars loaded to capacity came from each direction of the city, disgorging hundreds of students and teachers into the park for a day's picnicking. At the end of the afternoon, everybody, including lots of girls, gathered around the ball diamond for the big moment. You could feel the tension. It was students against teachers—for the record."

In this account, part fact and part fiction, Eddie Snyder (Isaac Davidson) remembered a famous game in August 1936:

> *Start with the students' team. I played left field. "Boogie" Auslander, second base, Eli Weinstein, first. Leonard Woolf, third base. Joe Pines was catching. Others played in different positions, shifting inning to inning. Benny and Harvey Pinson, Larry Etlin, Harvey Jerome. Mannie Sklar, Victor Marder, Bill Saltzman and Arnold Weiner. The teachers' team included Louis Schwartsman, Sidney Esterson, Simon Bugatch, Harry Tchack and Koppel Weinstein.*
>
> *The game see-sawed back and forth for the first three innings. By the fifth inning the teachers were ahead 5–4, and that is when, in the bottom of the sixth, the students loaded the bases for one of the best hitters they had, Ben Pinson* [Southwest]. *He worked the count to 3-and-2, and then hit the ball so far and so high it landed somewhere in Gwynn Oak Park but out of our playing area. The score was then 8–5 in favor of the students.*
>
> *It stayed that way for another inning or so, and then the teachers hit a home run—8–6. The students didn't score in the eighth but the teachers tied it with two, and made the score 8–8. The teachers did not score in the top of the ninth, and it was up to the students to try and win it in the bottom of the ninth. Somebody walked and somebody got a bloop single, and we had men on first and third when the next two batters popped up. Two out.*
>
> *I got up with the bases loaded. I was not all that good a hitter but our coach, Dr. Esterson, told me to bunt it down the first base line. Somehow, I managed to do that, and the man on third, whoever he was, came running home. The students had won it, 9–8.*

So Dr. Kaplan turned out to be right: teach the students a little softball along with their studies and they will not only be better students but also better softball players. That is the lesson the teachers learned that long-ago day at Gwynn Oak in 1936.

Originally published as "Diamond Days," December 28, 2007.

Amusing Times at Carlin's Park

Up until the 1950s—as Baltimorean Barry Levinson makes vividly clear in *Liberty Heights*—certain aspects of life in Baltimore (neighborhoods, swimming pools, beaches and clubs) were, if not in law then in effect, "restricted." One could see signs and ads that read, "No Jews Allowed" and "White Protestants Only." But many Jewish families living in Northwest Baltimore in those years didn't mind particularly. They had Carlin's Park.

Carlin's Park was opened in the mid-1920s by John J. Carlin, who lived nearby at Cottage and Keyworth Avenues, as a "family place," sprawling across seventy acres that hugged Park Circle, where Park Heights Avenue met Reistertown Road. Incongruously, Mr. Carlin placed at the entrance to the park a two-story Chinese pagoda.

Throughout the year, Carlin's was all things to all people. In summer, it offered a sawdust midway with carnival-style games of chance, full of the lively chattering of enterprising pitchmen. Dr. Sylvan "Pet" Shane worked on the midway when he was a boy in the 1930s. He recalls:

> *I had a job with Phil Schoolnick—he was one of those carnival pros who, when he saw a couple come along, would leap out in front of them and snap their picture. He would produce the picture immediately, pulling it out of a solution that smelled like ammonia gone bad. If the couple liked what they saw, Phil upped the ante and invited them into his little studio for a sit-down shot. I was Phil's assistant, and for my labors, I got forty cents an hour.*

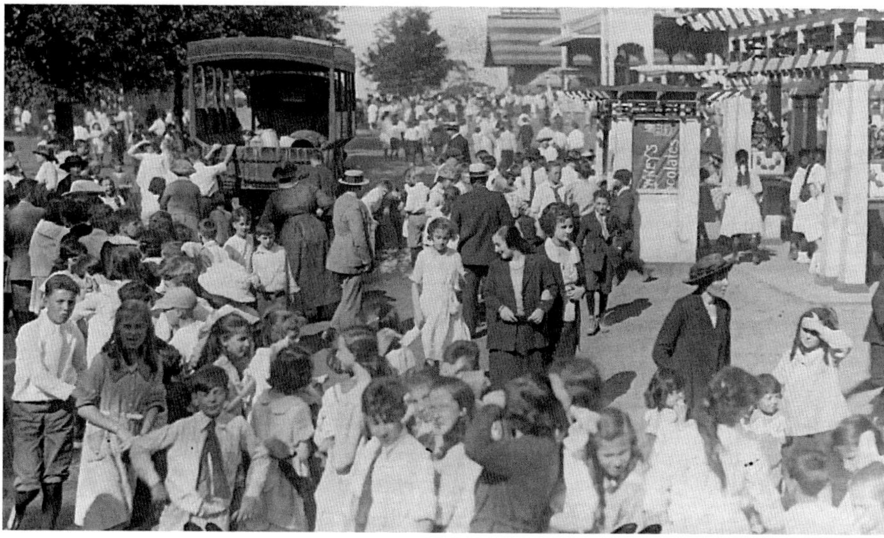

Patrons enjoy the midway at Carlin's Park, circa 1925. *Courtesy of the University of Maryland Libraries, Special Collections and Hearst Corporation, CP 4.2012.1.*

Then, there were the rides: Bug, Caterpillar, merry-go-round, a roller coaster, "Lindy Planes" and a penny arcade where a boy with five or six pennies could spend five or six hours—"winning" cowboy cards featuring the likes of Ken Maynard, Tom Mix and Buck Jones. In the arcade, too, a penny would let you go digging for treasure in a "claw" machine. By turning controls outside the glass case you maneuvered the claws around a particular gift (watches were the most attractive) buried in jelly beans. But the gifts were slippery and the claws were weak, and all a boy got for his efforts was a handful of stale jelly beans.

And then there was the fun house. The fun house was one of Carlin's most popular attractions. Kids couldn't stop talking about it days after they'd been through the place. The building itself was large, shapeless and barn-like. But inside was the stuff of childhood and adolescent joy. Bizarre attractions included a revolving disk about fifteen feet across that spun faster and faster until all of the kids holding on for dear life were thrown off; a sliding board two stories high; a rotating tunnel in which it was impossible to remain standing; mirrors that made the viewer look outrageously fat, thin, short or tall.

As a diversion, there was the titillating world of John Cypulski made possible by an arrangement of air hoses underneath the floor. Cypulski had a system that worked unerringly: as the girls walked along, they would

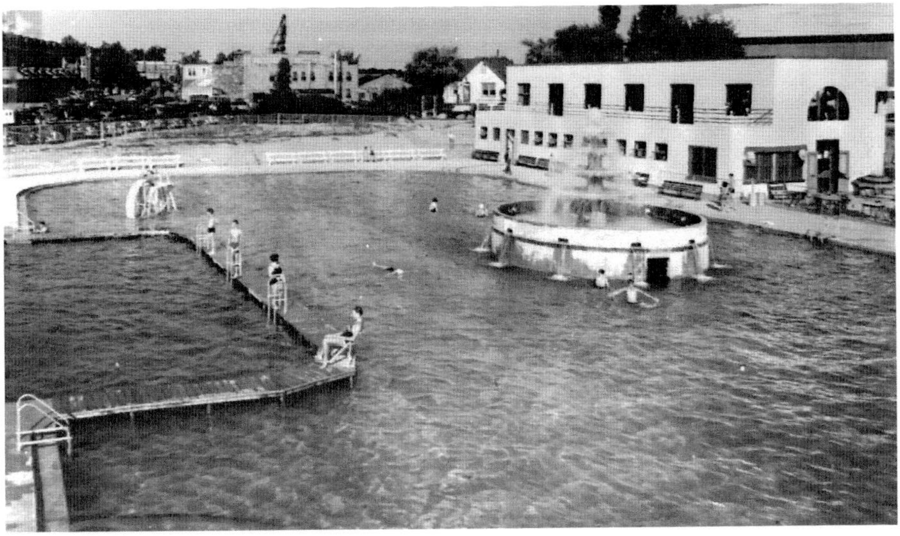

The pool at Carlin's Park was a popular feature because, unlike many other public and private pools in the city, it admitted Jews. Sundays held an especially strong draw as church attendance meant the pool would be relatively uncrowded. *Courtesy of the University of Maryland Libraries, Special Collections and Hearst Corporation, CP 4.2012.2.*

unknowingly pass over tiny and strategically placed holes in the floor. Through these holes came blasts of air perfectly timed to billow a girl's skirt up and out like an unfolding parachute. The embarrassed victim would grab at her skirt to hold it down—but always too late. That was the genius of John Cypulski, the operator of the device. "Pressing this button," he said, pointing to the control, "is an art." He explained that for the blast to do its work well, it had to appear a few critical seconds after the button was pushed; so he had to take into account how far the approaching victim was from the air hole, the speed of the victim's approach and the time it would take for the air to travel to its destination. It was a calculus Cypulski was proud of. "I never miss," he said. "I have perfect timing."

In summer, too, depending on the year, you could dance in Forest Gardens under the stars to the music of the big bands. But it was the swimming pool at Carlin's that endures in the history of Jewish Baltimore. At a time when many private recreational facilities were restricted, Carlin's pool was open. The crowd there was made up mostly of Jewish teenagers from the neighborhood of Rockrose, Hillsdale, Violet and Ulman Avenues and the streets off Park Heights and Reisterstown Road all the way to Pimlico. Charles "Charlie" Wagner was a lifeguard at the pool, and he recalls that "among the lifeguard crew, just about all Jewish, were Marvin Nachlas and Benson Schwartz, both now physicians, Morty Schwartz and Mannie Kalus."

In winter, depending on the year, the park offered boxing, wrestling and ice-skating. Iceland was the home rink of Baltimore's ice hockey team, the Clippers.

A memorable part of the Carlin's experience was the A&W Hot Shoppe, just to the south of the Chinese Pagoda entrance to the park. Although there was service inside, the big crowds, mostly from the high schools (City, Forest Park and Western), were out on the parking lot, inside their cars. Moments after you drove in, a uniformed carhop would come up to your car and attach a tray to the driver's window. She would take your order—grilled cheese, root beer floats, cement-thick milkshakes—return with your food and set it all on the tray attached to your car door. The A&W opened in 1932 and closed in 1956

But what accounted the most for Carlin's popularity among the Eastern European Jews of Northwest Baltimore was its completely "open door" policy—in a time of communal anti-Semitism, there was never a hint of anti-Semitism about the place. Far from it. Mr. Carlin himself lived in the neighborhood, in the heart of Baltimore's Jewish community, not too far from Shaarei T'filoh Synagogue and two blocks from Shaarei Zion Congregation.

Outside the park and huddled around the entrance was a small community of its own—Lapides Deli, Little Tavern hamburger, Park Circle Chevrolet and Davis's bicycle rental, Princeton Cycle, where a couple could rent a bicycle built for two and pedal through the leafy vistas of Druid Hill Park.

If you were among those who visited Carlin's in your youth, you can still hear the screams of the girls as the Mountain Speedway broke into a sudden wild descent. You can still feel the thrill of soaring out above the A&W in a Lindy Plane. And you can still see those newsboys' fires in Park Circle, aglow at the end of the day—and the end of a chapter in Baltimore history.

Originally published as "Amusing Times," September 27, 2002.

Back in the Haze: Jewish Sororities and Fraternities

Where are they now—the high school sororities and fraternities that were so much a part of the mystical and uncertain rite of passage for many Jewish teenagers up into the 1960s? Where now the bid, with its fierce overtones of social status? And the night of the big dance and the crinoline and the glitter and the corsages and the tension of adolescent struggle for one's place in the whole bewildering experience?

So important were high school sororities and fraternities in the lives of Jewish teenagers in the era, and so hurtful and devastating the adverse effect of rejection on those left out of the cliques, that in the mid-1960s, the Baltimore City Schools disbanded them. And even if they hadn't, the Jewish high school Greek letter societies would have faded away—a generation came along that rejected the very social status the institutions purported to offer. But though the party's over, the memories—good and bad—linger on.

Carole Brown Goldberg was in Sigma Theta Pi:

> *In my group, the aspiration for social standing started as early as the fifth grade. You hoped to get on a "track." I was in a club, Equinox, with Lois Hoffberger, Sue Shaivitz, Sally Sugar and our advisor, Rosellen Jacobson Fleishman, in Fallstaff Elementary. Then, in Garrison Junior High, we—Marilyn Reicher Levin, Claire Feldstein Sherman, Bonnie Speert Oletsky and Arlene Silberman Birnbaum—moved along the track into a junior high sorority, LOP—Lamda Omega Phi. Frankly, we looked for "cute girls" in the cafeteria. Moving along this same "exclusive" track,*

> *we went to Forest Park, and of course received bids to join Sigma Theta Pi. Dream come true! We had arrived at the top of the social ladder! Of course it was discriminatory, even cruel. Some girls who did not get a bid did not come to school the next day. But membership gave us confidence and allowed us to blossom.*
>
> *The biggest dance of the sorority calendar? Mu Sig's at the Chestnut Ridge firehouse! I wore plaid Bermuda shorts, red cashmere cardigan, a dickey, high socks and loafers! Although we required each member to put in a certain number of hours helping out at hospitals, in the end, it was all about status.*

Barbara Pollock Katz was in Sigma Theta Pi. "We held the Snowball Dance every Christmas Eve at the Phoenix Club. Beautiful affairs!" she says. "Flowers, tuxedos, formal gowns. Among our members were Joan Green Klein, Sarah Offit Abeshouse and Phyllis Cahn Finkelstein. I can remember one of the guys, my date, Harvey Kane."

Lin Reicher was active in Sigma Theta Pi in the early 1960s, along with friends Lisa Silver, Diane Rothberg and Sue Jacobs. "I was part of a later generation that included some who were beginning to see sororities as unhealthy influences," she says. "I was torn. My sister Marilyn had been active in Sigma Theta Pi five years earlier, so I was a legacy, yet I was among those who viewed the high school sorority-fraternity system as abhorrent. They had to go, and they did."

In the late 1940s, Phi Delta was the sorority of choice for Helene Land. "My friends were Adele Israel Loew, Shirley Shapiro Snyder, Ruth Wolpert [Rudick] and Phyllis Wolpert [Lifschutz] and Myra Tucker [Levy]. Although we had regular meetings, the focus was on our social life—in particular, the dances. We held them regularly at the Belvedere, Emerson and Stafford hotels."

Sonya Brenner Lansman was in Tau Beta Sigma, with Dorothy Barber Lipman, Raisa Roseman Livingston, Dolly Glassman, Pauline Handelsman and Joline Kaplan Sandler. Although the sorority held the usual dances at the downtown hotels, she remembers best the pajama parties: "We would take over a very large room of the Stafford Hotel and put in cots, wall to wall. We had a riotous time with the usual high school girls' pajama party pranks. It was wartime, and we visited the wounded at the Marine Hospital on Wyman Park Drive. I was caught up in the sorority friendships and went to the national conventions. Memories of my Tau Beta Sig days have lasted me a lifetime."

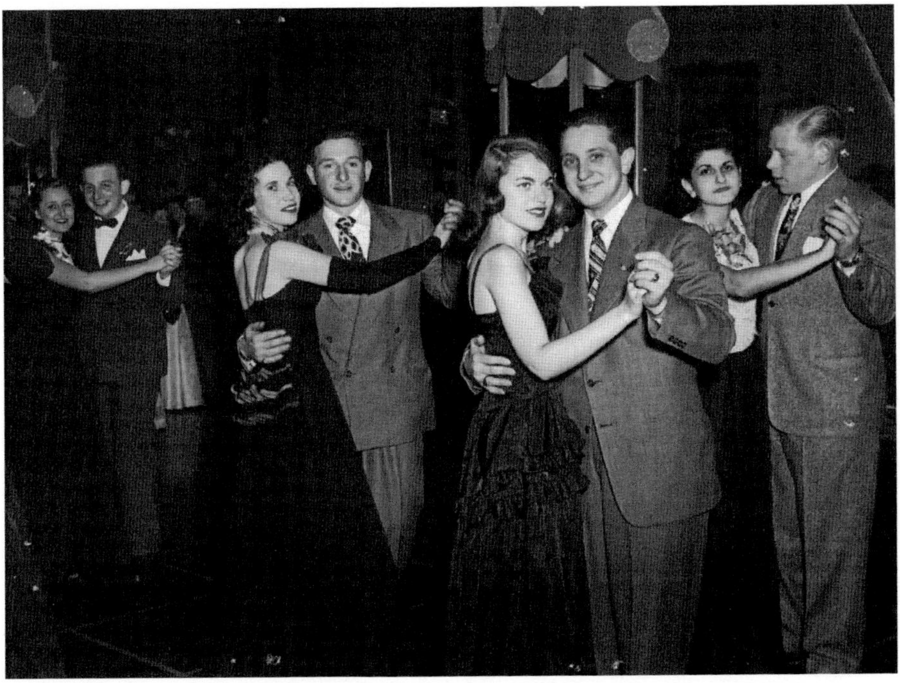

Members of a Baltimore Chapter of Tau Beta Sigma dance at the Hotel Stafford, circa 1950. While each of the ladies in this photo is identified by name, their dates are known only by affectionate (and not-so-affectionate) monikers. Pictured are Annette Cohen with "Cutie Pie," Pauline Handelsman with "Schlon," Raisa Roseman with "Eddie-the-Character" and Sonya Brenner with "Jerry-the-Jiver." *Gift of Dr. Virginia T. Pond, 1984.211.37.*

Says Barbara Shapiro, Sigma Theta Pi, "If you were in a clique, you had a date Saturday night. If you weren't 'in,' you didn't have a date—and you hid. The cliques really became ugly."

Carey Ries was president of Pi Tau Pi and recalls that, though some members were in the public schools—City, Poly and Forest Park—many, if not most, attended Park and Friends.

> *It followed, then, that a lot of our members were drawn from the Suburban Club—Lou Eliasberg, Stan Rothschild, Manny Dupkin, Joe Klein, Phil Wetzler. It isn't any secret that fraternities were selective in who they chose to let in—membership in a certain fraternity was a way of saying who you were, or who you wanted to be socially. That's the way it worked. They disbanded because the kids coming along didn't seem to care about any of that.*

Herb Kasoff (Forest Park, '58) chaired a reunion of the Mu Sigma fraternity at the Bonnie View Country Club in 2001:

> *More than 250 members attended! Mu Sigma had a large presence of public high school guys—City and Forest Park. Many of our members were prominent in high school. In 1956, both the president of City, Philip Weinstein, and the president of Forest Park, Jay Tarses, were Mu Sig. That was "status"! We gave dances at Frock's Barn where you'd see a lot of the sorority girls from Sigma Theta and Phi Delta. But it wasn't all fun and games, we did do a lot of volunteering at Levindale. By the 1960s Mu Sig, like all of the high school fraternities and sororities, dissolved.*

Jay Salkin was initiated into Upsilon Lambda Phi in 1953, when he was fourteen and a sophomore at Forest Park. He remembers:

> *ULP, as it was known, was competitive with Mu Sig, and I thought I was going to pledge Mu Sig until a friend, Billy Kogan in ULP, talked me into ULP, with Billy Kirk, Chuck Abelson, Keith Gasser, Billy Kolodner and Howard Cardin. The highlight of every year was a dance in a hall somewhere way out Greenspring Avenue. To gain admittance, a couple had to take the "kissometer" test. You'd kiss your date at the door and the "committee" would approve of it, and you were in. Our dates were mostly from Phi Lamda and Sigma Theta. The whole experience was about status—getting a bid and getting accepted into the "right" fraternity or sorority became everything. If you didn't get in or weren't invited to the dances, your peers thought of you as socially unacceptable—a terrible thing. Those days are gone and a good thing, too.*

There were many other Jewish high school fraternities and sororities, each a separate and complete circle of exclusivity, including the Sigma Pi Sigma sorority and Phi Beta and Alpha Phi Pi fraternities. But in retrospect, the Jewish high school sororities and fraternities were victims of the waning interest of young people in the very status the institutions offered. Who cared, they seemed to be asking, as the social prestige of sororities and fraternities went the way of debutante balls, social registers, coming-out parties and, in some measure, the country clubs.

Meanwhile, the public school administration saw the harsh caste system endemic to Greek letter societies as incompatible with the ethos of public schools, observing the toll the system was taking on students (rejecters and rejected alike). By the 1970s, most traces of Jewish high school sororities and fraternities were gone. And those days—the bids, the invitations, the dances, the dates, the pledge initiations, the status (for some) and the hurt (for others)—are now the stuff of memory, like a faded corsage left over from a Mu Sig dance.

Originally published as "Back in the Haze," October 24, 2003.

Fully Loaded: Sinning in a Sit-Down Deli

Joe Stowe, partner with Mark Horowitz of Suburban House restaurant at 911 Reisterstown Road, says, "If you think of the Jewish delis of, say, forty and fifty years ago—Nates and Leons, Sussman and Lev, Mandell's, Ballow's—with artery-clogging corned beef dripping fat, chopped liver loaded with *schmaltz* and a scattering of tables and booths along the wall, served by waitresses going crazy, owned by guys who trace their roots to old East Baltimore—if that is how you remember Jewish delis, well, in Baltimore, we are the last of them."

Joe is right about one thing; the place looks like the last of *something*—unrepentantly circa 1960 or earlier. Many there at breakfast, lunch and/or dinner have the look of what's left of the gang that rode the last No. 33 streetcar up Park Heights, went to the last show at the old Forest Theatre on a Saturday afternoon and jitterbugged at the last Jewish high school fraternity dance at City College. They say they have a problem with delis these days: the corned beef isn't like it used to be, the rye bread has no *kimmel* seeds and there are no pickle barrels around (although Attman's on Lombard Street still has pickle barrels). But if nothing at Suburban House is as good as it was in the delis of their growing up, what are all these *zaftig fressers* doing there in the first place? Simply put, *sinning*.

But Irving Lansman, whose A&L Foods has been a supplier to Baltimore delis for more than fifty years, says the number of sinners is dwindling. "People today are conscious of what they eat, and particularly wary of fatty foods, which is what deli is all about," he says. "Corned beef. Pastrami.

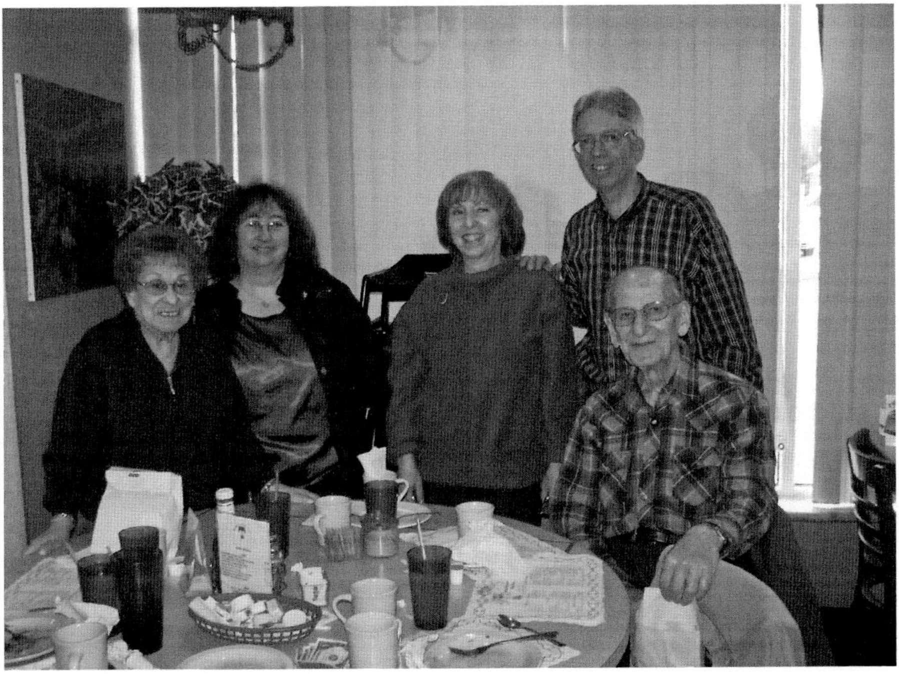

Lil Crane, Kira Lis, Linda Silverman, Tom Lis and Aaron Crane keeping the tradition alive with another delicious meal at the Suburban House in Pikesville, Maryland. February 2006. *Courtesy of Kira Lis, CP 15.2011.4.*

Salami. Hot dogs wrapped in bologna and dripping fat into the roll. So the number of people who patronize delis has shrunk, and so the number of delis to serve them has shrunk."

From appearances, the people who come into Suburban House must not have heard Mr. Lansman's doomsday view. When they sit down and scan the menu, their ravenous eyes gloss over. Out goes the diet.

Just ask Arlene and Robert Malech. They have driven to Suburban House from Columbia every Sunday morning since Suburban House has been in business. "It's the only deli left and only place I can get a good salami or chopped liver on rye," Arlene says. "It's this deli food that brings us here—you don't think we come here for the décor, do you? They could use some new carpeting."

At another table, Ronny Blumson and Herb Friedman are busy at work on overloaded platters of ham and eggs. Ronny says, "The portions are huge." Miriam and George Black seldom miss a Sunday morning at Suburban House. Miriam says, "We come for those great bagels and lox. It's the only place I know that serves hand-sliced lox."

The signature of a Jewish deli is, of course, the hot corned beef on warm rye, dripping with mustard. "We sell a lot of corned beef on rye," Mark says, "and a lot of stuff that is supposed to be bad—chopped liver, pastrami, kishka floating in gravy, knishes, potato pancakes, noodle kugel. Sure, we have thirteen different kinds of salads on the menu, but most of our customers come here to enjoy delicatessen—heavy with fat."

In and among the *fressers* addicted to fat-loaded deli is a minority that worries about it, and the Suburban House menu reflects that concern. Listed unobtrusively in and among the salami and the hot dogs are—may Sussman and Lev roll over in their graves!—Caesar salad and omelets made with cholesterol-free egg whites. "It's something to see," says Mr. Horowitz. "People order a fat-free omelet and then load it up with salami, and take a bagel loaded with cream cheese on the side! They watch their diets—until they order."

There is a certain quirkiness about the place. The waitresses seem to have been there forever—some have, for all the years Suburban House has been open. The décor is mostly plastic and in shades of the late 1970s. And then

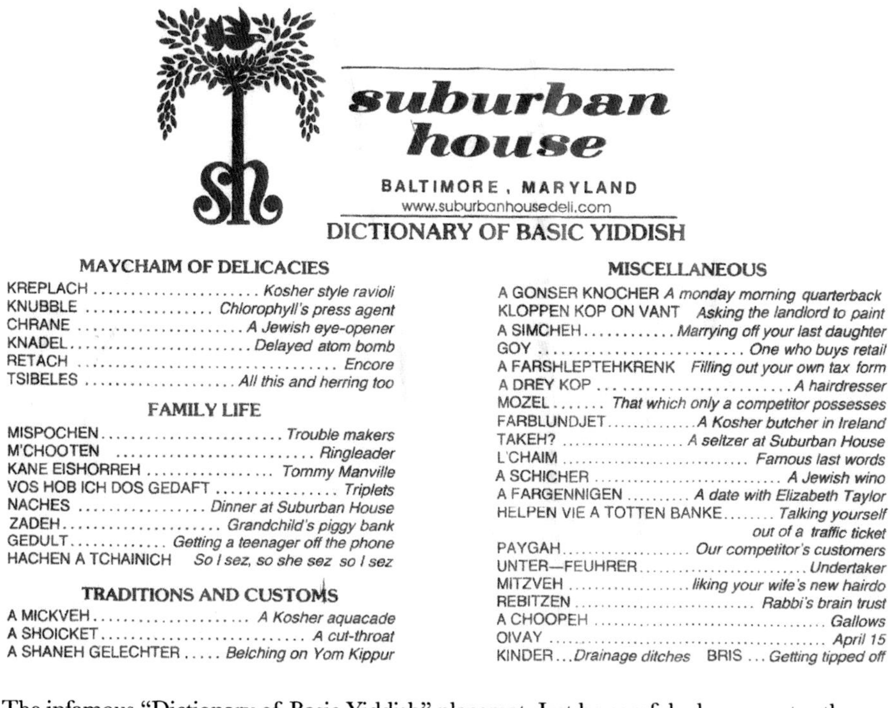
suburban house

BALTIMORE, MARYLAND

www.suburbanhousedeli.com

DICTIONARY OF BASIC YIDDISH

MAYCHAIM OF DELICACIES

KREPLACH .... *Kosher style ravioli*
KNUBBLE .... *Chlorophyll's press agent*
CHRANE .... *A Jewish eye-opener*
KNADEL .... *Delayed atom bomb*
RETACH .... *Encore*
TSIBELES .... *All this and herring too*

FAMILY LIFE

MISPOCHEN .... *Trouble makers*
M'CHOOTEN .... *Ringleader*
KANE EISHORREH .... *Tommy Manville*
VOS HOB ICH DOS GEDAFT .... *Triplets*
NACHES .... *Dinner at Suburban House*
ZADEH .... *Grandchild's piggy bank*
GEDULT .... *Getting a teenager off the phone*
HACHEN A TCHAINICH *So I sez, so she sez so I sez*

TRADITIONS AND CUSTOMS

A MICKVEH .... *A Kosher aquacade*
A SHOICKET .... *A cut-throat*
A SHANEH GELECHTER ..... *Belching on Yom Kippur*

MISCELLANEOUS

A GONSER KNOCHER *A monday morning quarterback*
KLOPPEN KOP ON VANT *Asking the landlord to paint*
A SIMCHEH .... *Marrying off your last daughter*
GOY .... *One who buys retail*
A FARSHLEPTEHKRENK *Filling out your own tax form*
A DREY KOP .... *A hairdresser*
MOZEL .... *That which only a competitor possesses*
FARBLUNDJET .... *A Kosher butcher in Ireland*
TAKEH? .... *A seltzer at Suburban House*
L'CHAIM .... *Famous last words*
A SCHICHER .... *A Jewish wino*
A FARGENNIGEN .... *A date with Elizabeth Taylor*
HELPEN VIE A TOTTEN BANKE........ *Talking yourself out of a traffic ticket*
PAYGAH .... *Our competitor's customers*
UNTER—FEUHRER .... *Undertaker*
MITZVEH .... *liking your wife's new hairdo*
REBITZEN .... *Rabbi's brain trust*
A CHOOPEH .... *Gallows*
OIVAY .... *April 15*
KINDER ... *Drainage ditches* BRIS ... *Getting tipped off*

The infamous "Dictionary of Basic Yiddish" placemat. Just be careful whom you try these phrases out on! *Courtesy of Samuel Stern, CP 7.2012.1.*

there are those paper placemats, which the regulars never even notice, that have been in use on the tables for years. One day in the 1980s, some non-regular did notice, got upset and talked to the media, and a small dust-up followed. The problem was that printed on the placemats is what purports to be a "Dictionary of Basic Yiddish."

For example, *mishpachah* (which means family) is defined in a wry manner as "trouble makers." The definitions, intended as insider humor for the regulars who "get it" happened to be seen by a non-regular who did not. The flashpoint: *goy*, "someone who pays retail." The complaint made it into the *Sun* and onto the local talk shows. Joe Stowe says he got calls from the media suggesting that he remove the placemats. Joe scoffs at the notion. "What? Admit that we were wrong? We weren't. It was good, acceptable, ethnic humor." The placemats are still there.

But if Suburban House is a model of the last surviving Jewish deli in Baltimore, it has not survived intact. It is not your father's Nates and Leons. Comparing menus of some of the delis that flourished long before Suburban House opened, you find a gustatory "then" and "now" history, pungent with traces of pickle brine. The Jewish delis along East Baltimore Street (Silverman's, the Vienna, Sussman and Lev) in the 1920s offered *helzel*, *pirogen* and *schav*. You will find none of these on the Suburban House menu, but you will find some low-fat and cholesterol-free items and a few very American dishes—spaghetti and meatballs, hamburgers, creamed chipped beef, a BLT.

By the way, Suburban House is not the first restaurant at its location—it is the fifth. The first to open at 911 Reisterstown Road was Mike and Jules in 1950; the second, in 1966, was the Suburban House (shortened to "S and H") owned by Sidney and Henry Cohen, who had been operating Cohen's deli at 1427 East Baltimore Street for many years. The third restaurant to operate on the premises (in 1984) was the New Suburban House, whose owner-operator was Jimmy Mexis. Six months later, the fourth restaurant to open in the location was the House of Pasta. In December 13, 1985, Joe Stowe and Mark Horowitz opened Suburban House.

There are any number of Sunday (and Saturday) morning regulars at the Suburban House. They sit at the same table, are served by the same waitresses and order the same things. One of the reunion gangs is made up of Nat Sandler, Sigmund Kassap, Nathan Goldberg, Sandy Seigel, Harold Hackerman, Lou Cohen, Stuart Danker, Mark Helman, Larry Kamanitz, Richard Manson, Larry Boltansky and David Uhlfelder. They are dieters—and order egg-white omelets. "Well," Mr. Kamanitz laments, "we've seen a lot of people die." At another booth are Rose Weistock, Alan Weistock and

Bruce Weingarten. Their plates are piled high with slices of noodle kugel, each slice maybe an inch thick.

There are *fressers* sinning in Suburban House at breakfast, lunch and dinner. "Our biggest seller for dinner by far is brisket, open-faced, smothered in gravy, with a stack of potato pancakes," says Joe Stowe. Asked how many calories in that platter, Joe says, "Forget it." Not far behind in popularity is the corned beef platter with potato pancakes. Next, blintzes, thick and heavy and piled high with sour cream.

People who come into Suburban House for deli seem to be making their own statement about Irving Lansman's notion about the declining popularity of deli food and weight and cholesterol, and the dwindling number of deli patrons and of delis. They are voting every time they make their choices on the menu. For them, it's corned beef on rye, don't hold the mustard, and a stack of potato pancakes piled high with sour cream.

And to hell with it!

Originally published as "Fully Loaded," May 25, 2007.

PART 5

Becoming American—and Making a Mark

Immigration is one of the great enduring themes of American history. Integral to that narrative is the struggle to get comfortable in America—to pick up its language, to catch its rhythms, to learn its stories and to be accepted. The ways into American life and culture were myriad. They included night schools, newspapers, libraries, English lessons, cooking classes and popular culture.

These stories reflect some of the many paths taken to feel "at home." But they also reflect an immigrant group growing steadily more confident of its place in America, contributing its own ingredients to the grand potpourri of local and national life and helping to shape a vibrant culture in the years after World War II.

Rhythm of America: Becoming American by Dancing to Its Music

On the early evening of May 27, 1910, the corner of Pratt and Bond Streets in old East Baltimore seemed unusually crowded. Couples arm-in-arm were entering the dance hall of the very popular Professor Harry C. Fink—to dance, to learn to dance, to sweeten a romance or perhaps to start a new one and, for a few precious hours, in pursuit of "becoming American," pick up the rhythm of American life by dancing to it.

Tonight at Professor Fink's tiny ballroom was special. It was the much-anticipated May Ball, and to enrich and enliven the evening, the professor was offering not just the usual dancing, but entertainment as well. The program for the evening listed "Lena Morstein and Ida Cohn, Song and Dance Artists," "Miss Rose Solomon, The Sweet Little Singer" and Miss Ida Fox as "The Dancing Doll."

As for the dances, patrons could take their choice: offered were the two-step, the waltz and the barn dance. No hint here of the *hora* or the *freilich* or the *Yiddishkeit* world their parents had left behind; this was the music of the new world they chose to come to.

We cannot know, so many years later, how these young Jewish couples felt that evening when they entered Fink's Hall, but we can guess: their spirits must have soared. Immigrants and the children of the immigrants only recently disembarked from the ships that brought them over from the *shtetls* of Lithuania and the Pale of Russia to Locust Point, they were consumed day and night with the hard work and endless hours of making a living.

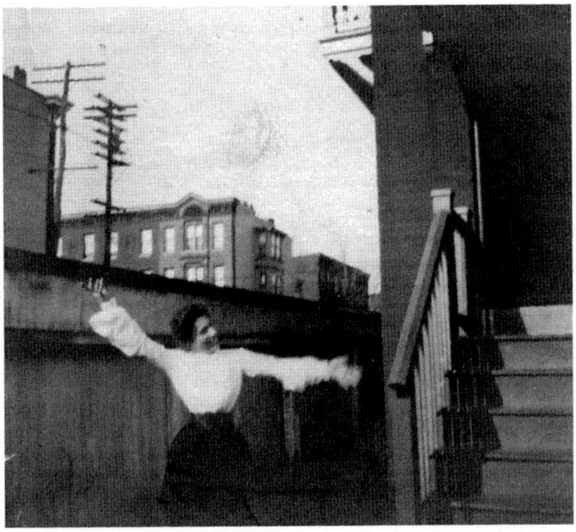

A young woman practices her dancing in the backyard of her Baltimore home, circa 1905. *Kraus Family Collection, 2003.53.385.*

Most, somehow or another, got jobs in Baltimore's burgeoning garment industry. They sewed in their homes and in the factories for Henry Sonneborn, Greif, Schoeneman and others. Many were peddlers. "Theirs was a hard life," according to historian Isaac Fein. With heavy packs, and over long distances, they carried pots and pans, needles and pins, clothing and tools up into Western Maryland for Baltimore's legendary entrepreneur and philanthropist, Jacob Epstein, and his Baltimore Bargain House. Small wonder these aspiring immigrants and children of immigrants looked forward to those few hours of music and dancing, and change of mood and scenery, to be had at Professor Fink's dance hall.

But out of the East Baltimore characterized by tenement life grew another East Baltimore, this one characterized by an unrelenting drive toward upward mobility, to prosper, to shed the opprobrium of old country greenhorns—in short, to "become American."

That is why, by the early 1900s, the families had turned their considerable energies to learning the language of trade and of social intercourse, to mastering crafts, businesses, the professions and generally easing their way into mainstream America. Many, but surely not all, wanted to become comfortable with American art, politics, philanthropy and pop culture. If money was scarce, aspiration was not. Sons of tailors, butchers and junkmen were encouraged to become doctors, lawyers and teachers. Jewish East Baltimore in 1910 was more than a neighborhood of tiny row houses, of sidewalks spilling over with cages of chickens, of pushcarts and storekeepers. It was a dream factory.

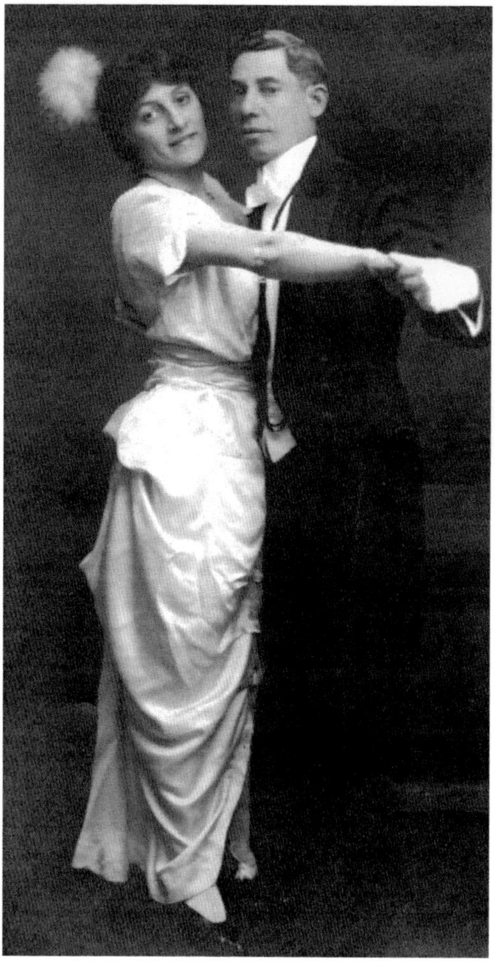

Professor Fink dancing with his wife at the height of his fame as a teacher of American dance. *Photo courtesy of Carole Ellin.*

Organizations were formed that would allow for facile transit into "America." Chapters of the B'nai B'rith and literary associations formed. Brith Shalom announced that its objective was to "improve on their own lonesome life in the newly adopted country." There were courses in American culture to enroll in, social clubs and dances at the Jewish Educational Alliance to be part of. This population of emerging immigrants was in a cultural exodus out into the non-Jewish world. They went Sundays to picnic and swim at Bay Shore Park, and they were taking the all-day excursion boats across the Bay to the amusement park and bathing beaches of Tolchester.

And that is why, on the evening of May 27, so many young Jewish couples were making their way over to Pratt and Bond Streets to the dance hall of Professor Harry C. Fink, there to dance to the siren music of America—the "Golden Medina," as they called this new country—and so to live their parents' and grandparents' dream that their children should "become American."

And what of the dream master himself, Professor Harry C. Fink? We are indebted to Carole Beerman Ellin (the wife of Dr. Morton Ellin), and her cousins Celeste Nader and Charlotte Peltz, for inheriting a cache of documents that tell the professor's remarkable story.

He was born in New York, the son of Solomon and Cecelia Fink, and came to Baltimore when he was seven. When he finished his schooling, he did not gravitate to the usual callings for young Jewish men of his times—storekeeping, sales, peddling, retailing, law, medicine or education. Instead, because he liked dancing, he decided to teach it, alone among his peers, to a population of working immigrants who, concerned with just trying to make a living, could hardly be thought of as being interested in dancing.

Perhaps they were interested because he did not teach the immigrants the *hora* or the *freilach* or the Middle Eastern dances (which would later become Israeli); he taught them mazurkas, polkas, waltzes, the European Schottische and the American Barn Dance. He had a sense that his pupils were not interested in the nostalgia of their immigrant culture, the sadness of life and the chronicle of suffering, but rather in the music of America and the rhythms of hope, freedom and love.

He met often with Arthur Murray (born Murray Teichman on New York's Lower East Side), America's dancing master, and brought Murray's American-style dancing into his own teachings.

When he died in 1935, Professor Fink was survived by his wife, Katy; daughters Ida May Fink Peltz and Madeline Beerman; two brothers, Frank and Jacob Fink; and two sisters, Lillian Fink and Helen Pifferling. He is buried in Hebrew Friendship Cemetery.

But Professor Harry C. Fink had many survivors beyond family—names unknown, but those who made up the immigrant East European Jewish neighborhood of East Baltimore in the early 1900s, all struggling to make it in America through the uncertain passage from old country "greenie" to Baltimore American, and so came to the tiny ballroom at Pratt and Bond Streets that long-ago night of May 27, 1910. They were looking to become American through its music and the dance, and the professor was only too happy to show them the way.

Originally published as "Rhythm of America," October 22, 2004.

All in the Family: Showtime at the Elektra Theater

On the Saturday afternoon of January 5, 1918, crowds were gathered on the sidewalk in front of 1039 North Gay Street, forming a line at the box office in front of the Elektra movie theater. They were there to see the *The Fisherman's Granddaughter*, which was much advertised and widely talked about.

In the darkened theater, the patrons quickly filled the 150 seats and sat waiting to cheer the heroes and boo the villains. They did not have to wait long; movies were silent, fifteen minutes in length, and management scheduled them close together. For that fisherman and his granddaughter in the featured movie (and her no-account husband), it was show time—Saturday afternoon at the Elektra, circa 1918.

Right on schedule, the screen came alive with flickering light and shadows. People moved about to the accompaniment of piano music (for a chase, the frenetic "William Tell Overture"; for a love scene, the breathless "*Claire de Lune*"). The actors "spoke"; their words appeared on the screen in bold letters, and their lips moved, but the audience was not fooled. The voices were of the "talkers," standing off to the side of the screen, reading from a script.

Among the Elektra's talkers were, according to the family's archivist, Richard Millhauser, all of the members of Moses Millhauser's family: Moses himself, age fifty-four, the sole owner; his wife, Flora (Adler), forty-eight; and their three children, Herbert, twenty-one; Gertrude, twenty-five; and David, twenty-six. In the day-to-day operation of the Elektra, the ticket-takers, the ushers, all of the voices of the on-screen performers, the janitors who opened

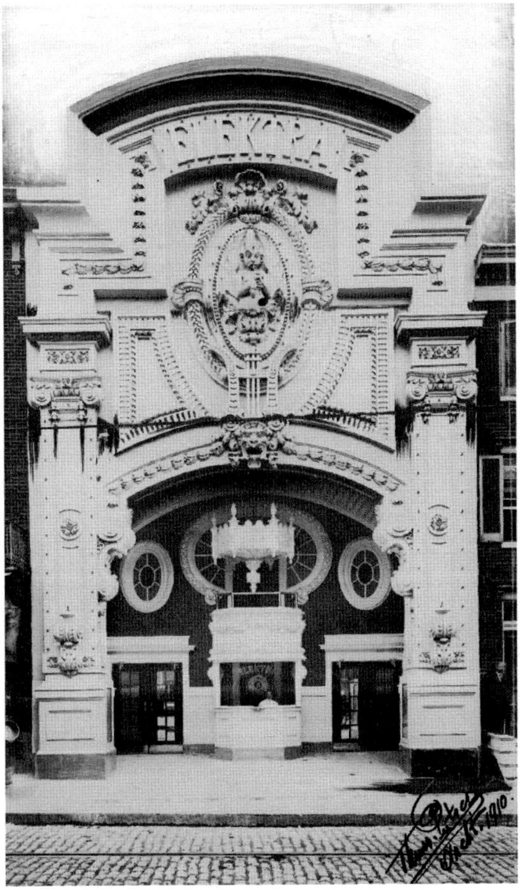

Façade of the Elektra Theatre, 1910. Patrons lined up outside the box office to get a taste of the American entertainment that the theater offered. *Gift of Richard Millhauser, 1991.133.4.*

the place, cleaned it and closed it—all of these tasks were performed by the Millhauser family. The theater could have been called "the Millhauser."

The plot of *The Fisherman's Granddaughter* was unapologetically sentimental, designed to bring tears to the eyes. In a resort, a vacationer falls in love with the granddaughter of one of the locals. Grandfather disapproves, so the couple elopes. Five years later, deserted and penniless, the hapless granddaughter comes home—with her baby. Grandfather forgives, and everyone embraces and lives happily ever after. The voice of the traitorous husband was Herbert Millhauser; of the grandfather, David Millhauser; of the hapless girl, Gertrude Millhauser.

The movie that played at the Elektra the week before was *The Wrong Man*, in which a young woman is pursued by a lascivious philanderer. She takes refuge in her home and hides in a closet. By coincidence, a plumber is working in the house, and she asks him to protect her. The girl's husband comes home, sees the plumber, assumes the man is his wife's lover and beats him up. The voice of the philanderer was Herbert Millhauser's; of the young lady, Gertrude Millhauser; of the husband, David Millhauser.

Her Adopted Parents had played at the Elektra a few weeks earlier. A poor and elderly couple are headed to the poorhouse and a tearful separation from one another. Out of nowhere, and by the strangest coincidence, a wealthy young woman presents herself, is moved by their plight, takes them into her home and adopts them, much to everyone's happiness. The voice of the old man was David's; of the wife, Gertrude's; and of the wealthy young rescuer, Flora's. The Millhausers, on occasion, used outsiders as voices—the names of Margaret Matthews and Robert North show up in the archives.

The immigrant Jews of old East Baltimore in the audience were completely taken in by this totally American entertainment form. Though there was at this time Jewish ("Yiddish") theater (the Bijou, the Princess and Blaney's, and Yiddish actors Boris Thomashevsky, Joseph Schildkraut, Maurice Schwartz and Molly Picon were in town often), there were no "Jewish" movies. These would be shown beginning in 1926 at the Folly, Fallsway and Baltimore.

To the population in East Baltimore, largely of Yiddish-speaking immigrants, American movies were both entertainment and, at the same time, instructive—an appealing and effortless way to learn English and become American.

The Elektra had stiff competition: the Gem on East Baltimore Street; the Dunbar on North Central Avenue; the Palace on South Broadway; the Cluster at 303 South Broadway; and the Teddy Bear on East Baltimore Street. Other forms of recreation, such as dance halls and rallies for Zionism and other causes, also drew attention. Attending Yiddish theater, the immigrants would become enveloped in the culture of the Old Country; attending Zionist rallies, they would become caught up in Jewish nationalism; but watching the fifteen-minute three-reelers on a Saturday afternoon at the Elektra, they would become American.

Originally published as "All in the Family," April 27, 2007.

Baltimore's Jewish Drum and Bugle Corps

During World War II and through the mid-1940s, it became a happy commonplace for many Baltimore neighborhoods to welcome returning veterans with a block party. A street would be shut off to vehicular traffic at both ends, creating a pedestrian mall. Tables would be set out, refreshments offered and speeches proffered. Sometimes there would be dancing in the streets to a small pick-up band of neighborhood kids that could play "Don't Sit Under the Apple Tree" reasonably well. In the Jewish neighborhoods of Park Heights and Forest Park, as well as in the neighborhoods of East Baltimore—Highlandtown and Patterson Park—more often than not, the signal to open the day's festivities would be the sounds of the blaring bugles and pounding drums of what was Baltimore's first, last and only all-Jewish drum and bugle corps, the Maccabean Squadron of the Sons of the American Legion, as they arrived on the scene.

And what a scene, wherever they made their appearance! Enough to make the heart skip a beat! Twenty-four boys (and one girl—more about her later) strong; six columns of four, sixteen buglers, two bass drummers, four drummers, two cymbal players, all resplendent in their uniforms of light blue pants, dark blue shirt, yellow tie, blue overseas cap (or, depending on the year, blue pants, maroon coats and white Sam Brown military belts) and led by a strutting young majorette.

They were all under seventeen years of age. They had all mastered the talent of coaxing the four notes of a bugle to the accompaniment of drums into wondrous music—and they were all Jewish.

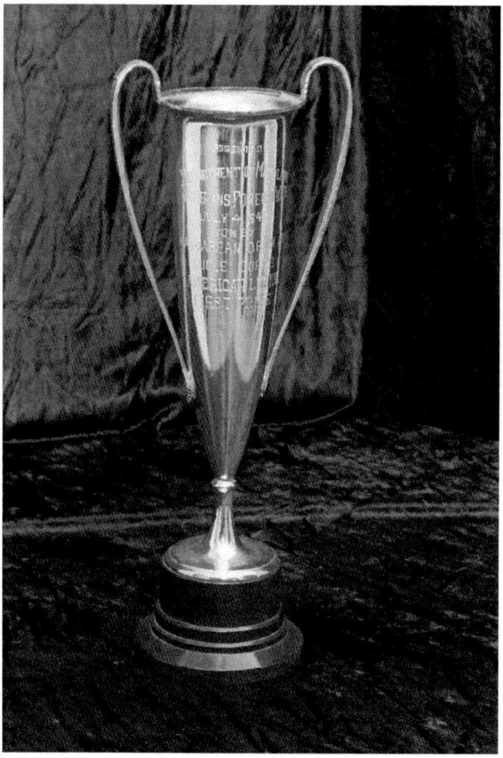

While an all-Jewish drum and bugle corps in Baltimore may have been an anomaly, it was a talented oddity. On Independence Day 1942, the Maccabean Squad earned a First Prize trophy from the Veterans of Foreign Wars. *Gift of Mrs. Beverly Moses, 1991.144.4.*

No official list of the entire Corps membership exists—the Corps was formed in 1936 and did not disband until 1946 and probably involved over the years as many as one hundred boys—but certain alumni and alumnae of the old Maccabean Corps are still around to share the memories. To mention some but surely not all: Hillel Aarons, Maurice Burman, Gilbert and Irwin Cohen, Joel and Morty Davis, Daniel Fink, Joel Hurwitz, Daniel Marcus, Mannes Shalowitz, Merrill Skolnik and Robert Swerdlin. Sadly, Melvin Adelman was killed at Iwo Jima and Hersch Davis at St. Lo in Europe.

The Maccabean Drum and Bugle Corps came into being in the 1930s as a response to the need of Jewish war veterans of World War I to reaffirm their patriotism. Beginning in the late 1930s and into the early 1940s, the world was gearing up for war; American Legion posts, as an expression of and an outlet for patriotism, were flourishing. In this martially charged atmosphere, it was not surprising that the Maccabean Post, composed of Jewish war veterans, would launch the Sons of the American Legion (SAL).

What was surprising was the founding, as an affiliate group of the SAL, of the Maccabean Drum and Bugle Corps. Considering that the other drum and bugle corps were in such gentile neighborhoods as Hamilton and affiliated with churches all over town (not synagogues), a Jewish drum and bugle corps was an anomaly. There had never been one.

About the "one girl": When the Corps was formed it was led, with much strutting and baton twirling, by Eleanor Block. When she left the Corps in

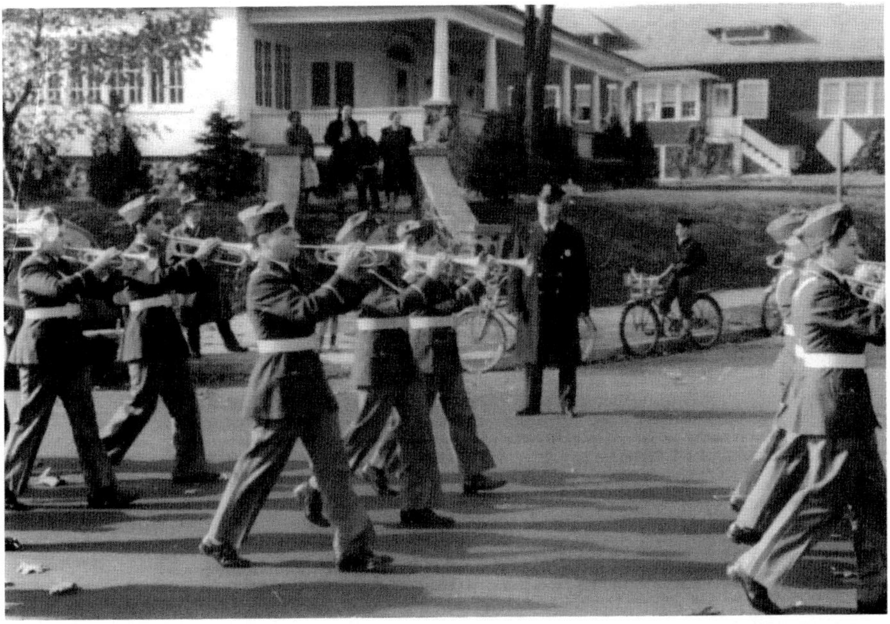

The Maccabean Squad turns out in full regalia, dazzling the neighborhood with its rendition of "You're a Grand Old Flag," circa 1942. *Photo courtesy of Daniel Fink, 2003.91.2.*

1936, her place was taken by eight-year-old Donna Oshry [Highstein] of PS 61 and PS 49; Western High School, 1946; and Goucher College, 1950. She explains how and why:

> *My father, Morris, was a member of the Maccabean Post of the American Legion, just at the time when an opening for drum majorette opened up. My father suggested I try out for the position. I didn't know anything about how to be a drum majorette, and nobody taught me. I just did what I thought drum majorettes were supposed to do. I strutted, I twirled my baton. My mother made my uniform. It was white satin, with gold buttons down the front. The high point of my majorette career was leading the Corps onto the field at old Municipal Stadium! I was the majorette for the Corps until 1943 when I was fifteen. Sixty-some years later, I can still remember hearing the Corps play "You're A Grand Old Flag."*

The beginnings of the Corps go back to the formation of the Maccabean Post American Legion on December 8, 1931. At a meeting two years later, the post commander, Ben Wolfson, urged the post to establish a Sons of the

American Legion and gain the distinction of being the first one in Maryland. And the next year, member Emanuel Gorfine announced that the Sons squadron had indeed been formed and was already meeting in the club room of the Trenton Democratic Club on Park Heights and Violet Avenues. The Sons would continue to meet in the gym of the Eutaw Place Temple.

In the next year, 1935, Chairman Harry Berman reported that the squadron members were at work organizing the sons into a drum and bugle corps, and on November 10, 1936, Morris Oshry announced that the drum and bugle corps was officially in rehearsal. Rehearsals were held in the gym of the Eutaw Place Temple, Shaarei Zion and Har Zion.

The Corps' first official public performance was March 17, 1938. It was part of the evening's entertainment for the members of Brith Shalom in the Brith Shalom Hall. Other performances followed, at carnivals, in the July Fourth parades in Dundalk, annually on Memorial Day at the Baltimore Hebrew Cemetery and at countless block parties.

Marty Lev was fourteen in 1940 when he joined the Corps. "My father was a member of the Maccabean Post, and he thought it would be a good idea if I joined. Being a big guy, they gave me a big bass drum to carry and pound out the beat. It weighed about twenty pounds—nothing for me to carry at the time. Joe Soistman was my instructor, and if I missed a beat he'd let me know about it." All three Davis brothers were in the Corps—Hersch (the oldest), Morty and Joel. "They taught me to play the bugle," Morty remembers. "I was told that it could play four notes, but I think I only learned to play one." He recalls marching with Whitey Hurwitz, Aaron Levy, Jerry Mandelberg and Stan Forschlager.

Merrill Skolnik, who was a young man in 1943 and captain of the SAL Squadron, reflects on the life and times of the Corps:

> *The boys of the Maccabean Drum and Bugle Corps grew to be men, most of whom remained in Baltimore and have taken their places as successful members of the community. In 1970, some thirty-five years after the Corps was founded, we held a reunion and reminisced about the old days, and the happy times the Corps had parading as Jewish members of the Sons of the American Legion. We had such good memories that we thought about joining ranks right there that very night and parading down the streets of Baltimore playing "You're A Grand Old Flag." But no one remembered to bring the instruments.*

Originally published as "Sounding Off," November 22, 2002.

Incubator of the Stars: Forest Park High School

Something big was going on the night of January 27, 1973, in the lobby of the Morris Mechanic Theater on Baltimore and Charles Streets. Men and women in their sixties were embracing, chattering and laughing and gathering around pictures hanging on the walls. The occasion was the fifteenth reunion of the Forest Park High School class of 1958. These were the graduates, and the pictures on the walls were of themselves from their 1958 yearbook.

But the occasion was more than a class reunion. The crowd was also here to honor one of their own, Kenneth Waissman, a 1958 Forest Park graduate and the producer of the smash Broadway hit *Grease,* scheduled to open in Baltimore at the Mechanic two nights later. The costume designer of the show was fellow Forest Parker Carrie Fishbein Robbins. Since its opening in New York five years earlier, *Grease* had become one of Broadway's most successful and longest-running shows. But this night, January 27, 1973, *Grease* and Waissman had come home to Forest Park High and to the Baltimore of the 1950s, where it all began. Joining him was fellow Forest Park alumna, Maxine Fox, who was his co-producer and whom he later married (and divorced).

Because it was coed, and the only high school in Northwest Baltimore that was, Forest Park, at Eldorado Avenue and Chatham Road, was arguably the school of choice for many Jewish boys and girls coming out of what were in those days "junior high school." (In the case of the Jewish community's Northwest Baltimore population, that meant Garrison Junior High School.)

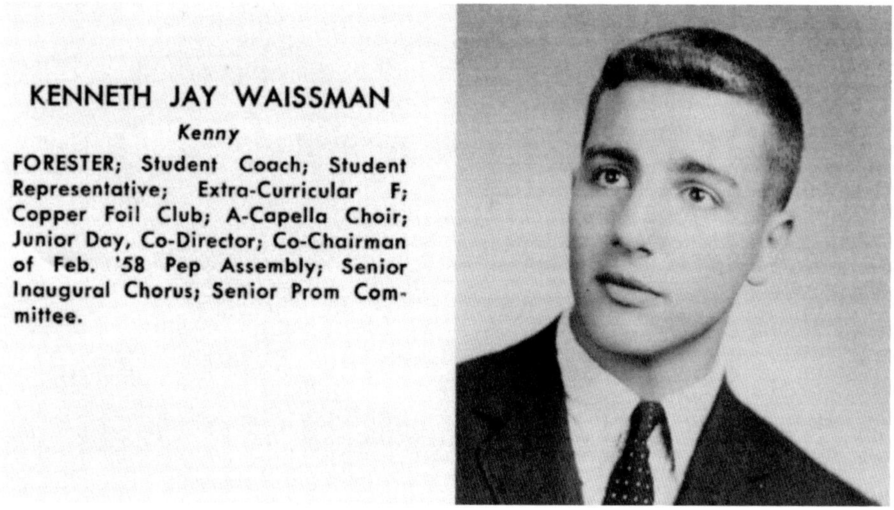

By graduation, Kenneth Waissman had already racked up a string of accomplishments. *The* Forester, *1958, CP 3.2012.1.*

The Forest Park High School they entered in the 1950s was, from its opening until the mid-1970s, all white and—to judge from the names—had a large population of Jewish students. Though prominent in student life, they did not dominate it, although Jewish high school fraternities and sororities were popular. Gary Huddles was active in the Mu Sigma fraternity. "We drew most of our members from Forest Park," he recalls. "In 1956, both the president of City, Phil Weinstein, and the president of Forest Park, Jay Tarses, were Mu Sigma."

In February 1958, the year that Mr. Waissman graduated, longtime principal Wendell Dunn still held the office. Veteran teacher Virginia Shaffer was head of the English Department; Rex Simms, of gym and athletics. Patricia Kane was president of the class; Jay Green and Sylvia Matz were vice-presidents. The senior prom was held on the night of February 8, 1958, at the Sheraton Belvedere. Ann Epstein and Anita Goldberg were co-editors of the *Forester*, the yearbook; the football team (the Foresters) were 4-0—Milt Lumsden was the coach, and Jack Hoppenstein was team captain. And under Ken Waissman's picture in the February 1958 yearbook, some hints at future stardom: "A Capella Choir, Pep Assembly, Senior Inaugural Chorus."

At first glance, the 1950s at Forest Park did not appear to be remarkable, but they were. In this decade, a quiet incubation seems to have been going on at the school, a yeasty fermenting that would only be recognized and understood years later. Forest Park High School was quietly giving birth to what would be the soaring, coruscating careers of some of America's best-known Jewish talent in American popular entertainment.

Barry Levinson graduated in the class of 1960, sort of. According to writer Allen Breed, "He stayed up all hours playing cards, hanging out at the Diner. He was crowned fraternity king at Forest Park because of his Ricky Nelson good looks." A friend of those days, Donald Saiontz, who also hung out at the Diner, said, "I worried about him." History has shown that he needn't have. Levinson went on, circuitously, to become an Academy Award winner and widely popular as writer-director of such super hit movies as *Good Morning, Vietnam*; *Tin Men*; *Avalon*; and *Rain Man*.

Mama Cass Elliot came into the world as Ellen Naomi Cohen. Born in Alexandria, Virginia, in 1941, she grew up in Baltimore and attended Forest Park High School. At the same time, she held down after-school jobs, successively, for the *Baltimore Jewish Times* and the classified department of the *Sun*. Classmate Rona Weintraub Hoffman, remembered her: "Ellen and I used to sit around the cafeteria and eat ice cream and sticky buns. One day she said to me, 'I've changed my name. From now on, I'm Cass Elliot.'" She changed her life, too. The next day, two weeks before graduation of the class of 1960, she dropped out of Forest Park and went to New York to try her luck in show business—with no more going for her than a few small parts in Don Swann's dinner theater, then operating in Owings Mills.

She went on to become one of the founding members of the Mamas & the Papas. On July 30, 1974, at the crest of her popularity, she came home to Baltimore to participate in Cass Elliot Day, a parade and welcoming ceremony held in her honor. The highlight of the occasion was when Mayor Schaefer personally awarded her the diploma she never got from Forest Park. When she died unexpectedly at age thirty-three, the *Sun* editorialized, "Few grads have honored Forest Park as well, and few have left such memorable music for the nation's young and not so young."

Jay Tarses was president of the class of 1957 and a member of the National Honor Society. He went on to become acclaimed writer/producer of, among many blockbuster television hits, the Carol Burnett, Bob Newhart and Tony Randall shows. Norman Steinberg was also in the class of 1957 and a member of the National Honor Society and, over a long and winding road, made it big as a highly successful comedy writer, best known for his work with Mel Brooks, with whom he wrote the classic *Blazing Saddles*. He also gave old classmate Herb Kasoff walk-on parts in several television shows.

Many alumni and alumnae of Forest Park who graduated before the 1950s and after have brought the school honor with their careers, toiling locally and establishing their considerable reputations—Hillary Kilberg, active in local theater and radio and TV advertising; Shirley Glass, a nationally respected psychologist; Alfred Coplan, prominent businessman and leading activist in Jewish communal affairs. But Barry Levinson, Kenny Waissman, Maxine Fox, Carrie Fishbein Robbins, Ellen Naomi Cohen, Jay Tarses and Norman Steinberg got out there where the lights were bright, and in one brief, shining decade, the 1950s, in some unexplained way, seemed to be preparing for careers that years later would light up the skies, leaving to the classes behind them their legacy of achievement in the world of entertainment.

Subsequent generations of Forest Park classes should be forgiven if they were not the equal of this remarkable group that made Forest Park a rich breeding ground of pop artistry in the 1950s. It was a tough act to follow.

Originally published as "Top Grade Talents," September 24, 2004.

Hugs and Knishes: The Jewish American Festivals

It had not happened before, and it hasn't happened since—up to a quarter of a million people gathered in one vast fairground in Baltimore to express and celebrate the idea of being Jewish. The years were from 1979 through 1992. The fairgrounds varied but included Baltimore's Inner Harbor, Druid Hill Park and the parking lot in the Owings Mills Town Center. Whatever else the festivals did or did not accomplish, they brought the community together—to sing, to dance, to eat, to shop, to *schmooze*, to "people watch" and to argue. You had to have been there.

Sol Goldstein was the founding chairman of the committee in 1979 that organized the festival and managed it to what, by any measure, was a resounding success. But that success, according to Mr. Goldstein, was earned the hard way:

> *Any time you attempt to bring together so many disparate and vocal Jewish groups all functioning within the larger Jewish community, you are going to be presented with challenges to reconcile. And there were.*
>
> *For example, a problem came out of nowhere. It turned out that many of our vendors were selling Pepsi-Cola, which seemed to be innocent enough. But this was during the time when Pepsi-Cola was being attacked because the company, under pressure from Arab countries, which threatened to boycott Pepsi throughout the Arab world, wouldn't sell Pepsi in Israel. And it was the sense of many Baltimore Jews that Pepsi-Cola had capitulated. But with help from Rabbi Herman Neuberger of Ner Israel Rabbinical*

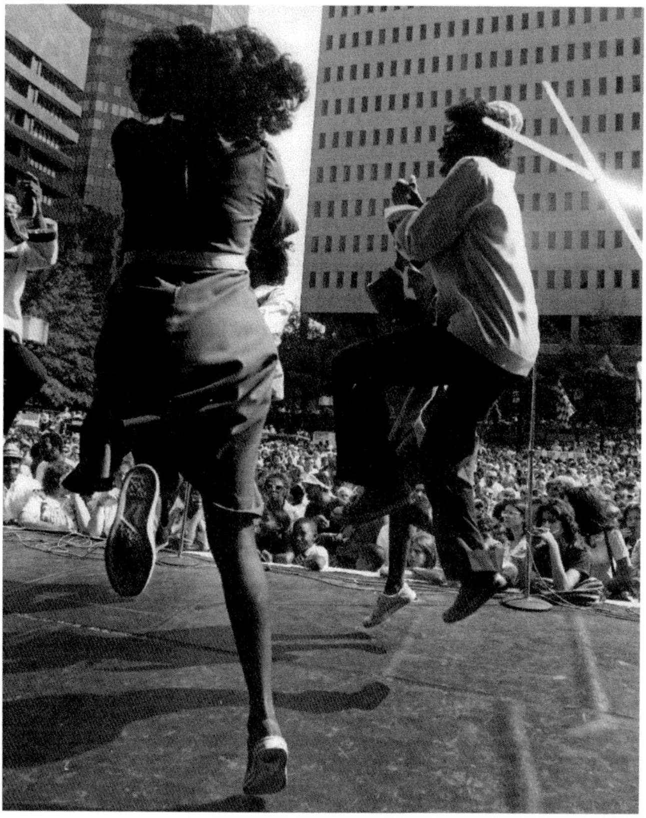

Performers dancing at the Baltimore Jewish American Festival, 1976. *Gift of Ed and Judy Oppel, 1992.205.59.*

College, we developed a stand on the matter—the Jewish merchants were entitled to sell Pepsi at the festival, particularly since a Jewish family, the Lapideses, were the local bottlers. But the matter actually got physical, there was pushing and shoving before it was all over.

In the Jews for Judaism booth, tempers flared, as members of "that counter-missionary" group confronted the highly vocal Jews for Jesus contingent. Melvin Berger and Michael Rosenberg organized the booth as a Jewish answer to the Jews for Jesus booth, whose supporters had previously passed out literature in and around the festival grounds. "We *should* give out literature, too," Berger told a *Baltimore Sun* reporter. "Our aim is to keep as many Jews as Jewish as possible, especially the young people seeking fulfillment through alternative religions."

When Israel Hirschberg, who worked in the Jews for Judaism booth, learned that Christian missionaries were passing out literature according to a report in the *Jewish Times*, he went on the offensive. Recalls Mr. Goldstein: "Knowing that the missionary literature was kept in the trunk of evangelicals' cars, Mr. Hirschberg threatened to glue the doors shut unless they stopped the distribution." They did. Mr. Goldstein continues:

> *There were other questions of kashrut to be argued through. We had to close down a french fries stand because it was proved that they were not preparing their fries according to kashrut. And, too, there was the matter of the piña coladas. Certain rabbis were concerned about the ingredients of the drink, and we had to research all the way to Puerto Rico to have the ingredients validated as kosher.*
>
> *It was not unlike a situation we dealt with in the 1987 Rally for Soviet Jewry in Washington. Some Orthodox Jews protested the appearance of Mary Travers in the Peter, Paul and Mary group we had booked as our lead entertainers. They objected to a woman up on the stage entertaining men.*
>
> *But the confrontations were small and didn't really diminish the community's joy and pride in the larger festival itself, and many if not most attending were unaware of any of the management problems. A visitor was caught up, even overwhelmed, with the faith and the fun, and the continuing non-stop carnival of the Baltimore Jewish community's Yiddishkeit, its lifestyle, and its intramural and highly visible differences on stage for all the world to see.*

At the Lubavitch booth, the hosts enabled people to try on *tefillin*, or phylacteries, and say the appropriate prayers. Rabbi Shmuel Kaplan, the local Lubavitch representative, said that hundreds of men came by the booth and put on *tefillin.* So many came that Rabbi Kaplan asked a *Jewish Times* reporter, "Where did you ever see a line of people waiting to put on *tefillin*?" Then there was Moshe the Camel, lending an authentic desert touch, courtesy of the Zionist Youth Group. Moshe, a costumed look-alike with two young men inside providing the four legs, had a sign on his tail: "Follow me to Israel."

The Etz Chaim Center for Jewish Studies offered a quickie course in Basic Judaism and Hebrew. "Students" were presented with a free book, "Rosh Hashanah-Yom Kippur Survival Kit."

And music and dancing! There was "The Rockin' Rabbi," Avraham Rosenblum, self-proclaimed leader of the "World Famous Diaspora Yeshiva Band," and "Dr. Laz and the Cure"—a musical group formed at the time of

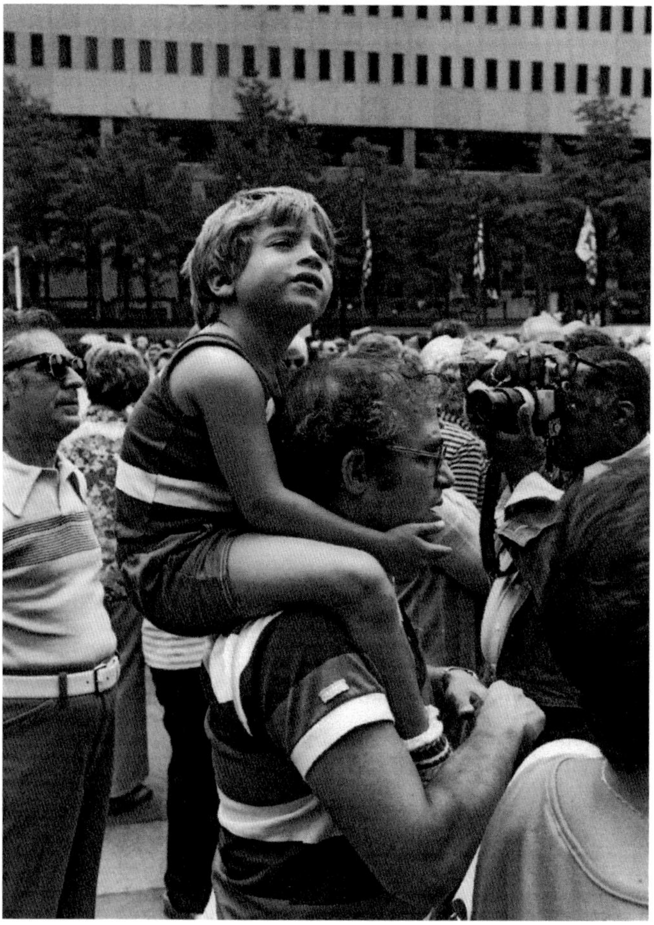

Father and son take in the sights at the 1976 Jewish American Festival. *Gift of Ed and Judy Oppel, 1992.205.67.*

the 1991 Crown Heights riots, featuring, symbolically, the dancing together of blacks and Chasidic Jews.

Food! Everywhere! All of the time! Falafel, *knishes*, *pirogen*—and *cholent*, offered one year by the volunteers from the National Council of Synagogue Youth. Their carnival cry: "Come taste the only truly Jewish food at the festival!"

Looking back on the festivals a full decade after the last one in 1992, Sol Goldstein reminisces:

> *These festivals could not be put on by one person. There were lots of wonderful people who gave of their time and goods. Much of the entertainment was obtained by Ira Westridge. Mel Berger gave generously*

of his money and material. Ellen Lightman, Erwin Burtnick and Shmuel Kaplan were tremendously helpful.

The festivals were started by a group put together at the Baltimore Jewish Council. Stanley Sollins was the executive director at that time. I was asked to be the chair, and I accepted. Staging the festivals was an exercise in Solomonic diplomacy. We never had problems, although people thought we did. We had challenges. Debate, exchanging points of view, reconciling differences of opinion—that is what the Talmud is about, and that is what the Jewish festival was about, and if they have it again, that is what it is going to be about—and should be. Knishes, with a little Talmud on the side.

Originally published as "Hugs and Knishes," September 26, 2003.

The Jews of Prime Time

David Zurawik, television critic for the *Sun* and author of the book *The Jews of Prime Time*, made a well-documented case that the television networks, though Jewish owned, eschewed any Jewish presence on camera—going so far as to reject any hint of Jewish dialect, food or lifestyle (*The Goldbergs* being the one short-lived exception). Dr. Zurawik's findings led me to examine local television in the same period and to the discovery that the parallel histories proved to be entirely different.

Locally, there were any number of entertainers, known well in the community as Jewish, and an atmosphere that accommodated, even welcomed, diversity. An observer comparing can only conclude that all of those actors and actresses and screenwriters up against anti-Semitism in New York–based national TV should have come to Baltimore.

***

It is about 8:45 a.m. on a Tuesday in the late 1950s. Half a dozen mothers and some fathers with their five-year-olds in hand are milling about the lobby of WAAM-TV (later WJZ) on Television Hill. These mothers, fathers and children are nervous. They are going to be on television! Specifically, on Miss Nancy's *Romper Room*, where each child hopes to prove to the world that he or she is a "Do-Bee." And for five-year olds in Baltimore of that era, that was a very important thing to prove. At 9:00 a.m., the families were ushered into the studio, and the children took their places in a kindergarten setting. Miss Nancy was the teacher, and before long Miss Nancy had the group playing the Do-Bee game. For example, Miss Nancy taught, "Do-Bee a milk drinker," "Do-Bee a room straightener," "Do-Bee a bed maker." But "Don't-Bee a shoe dropper, a street crosser or a nasty tongue."

Do-Bee posters were all over the studio walls, picturing the Do-Bees as merry and charming bumble bees. For a parent or child after the Do-Bee experience, life was never the same. A mother in the course of a day would be forever playing the Do-Bee game to suit her needs—like "Do-Bee a patient little girl while Mommy is on the phone"—borrowing creatively from Miss Nancy. Matter of fact, the word "Do-Bee," meaning the gentle coaxing of a child to do your bidding, became part of the language of kids and parents in the Baltimore of the '50s.

"Miss Nancy" was in real life Nancy Goldman Claster, a member of Har Sinai Congregation. She was raised in an Orthodox Jewish family and the wife of Bert Claster, who had worked for the Hippodrome Theater before he went into television production. Nancy Goldman was one of at least half a dozen television personalities popular in Baltimore at that time who were Jewish.

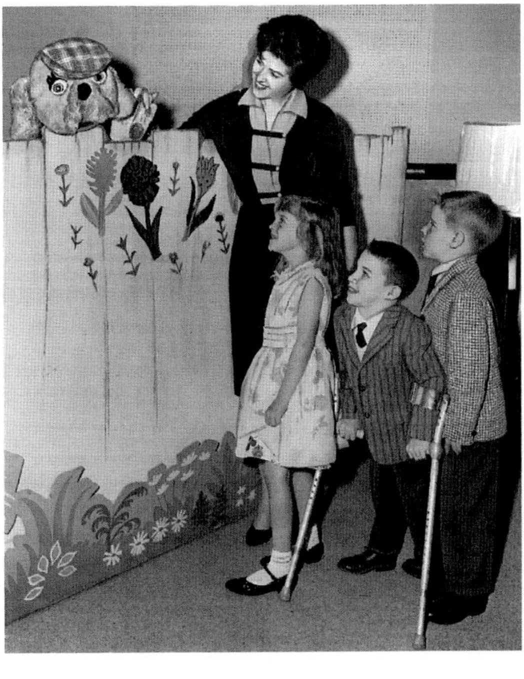

"Miss Rhea" and Sunshine the puppet visited students at Pleasant Plains Elementary School on May 3, 1962. *Courtesy of the University of Maryland Special Collections, Baltimore News American Collection and Hearst Corporation, CP 4.2012.8.*

Rhea (Mermelstein) Feikin traces her career in television back to a librarian in her old neighborhood. It was she who told Rhea's mother that ten-year-old Rhea had a promising career in theater. Rhea wound up in Children's Theater and, while still in high school (Forest Park, 1952), was on Tommy Dukehart's WAAM talent show *High Time*. Not surprisingly, in college (University of Maryland, 1956), Rhea became a speech therapist and after graduation went to work in the Baltimore City School System. It so happened that, at the time, the system was looking for the appropriate person to host a new television show, providing education in speech improvement. Rhea volunteered. "I conceived the format, wrote it, hosted it and created the 'teacher'—'Betty Betterspeech.'" The career of one of Baltimore's most enduring television personalities was launched.

Rhea's performance as Betty Betterspeech caught the attention of WBAL executives Brent Gunts and Sid King. "They asked me to work on a children's program," Ms. Feikin recalls, "and we came up with 'Miss Rhea and Sunshine.' It was a puppet show with Cal Schuman and ran for at least ten years on WBAL–TV." Ms. Feikin became popular, too, as a "weather lady," with help from a puppet named JP.

Royal Parker (Pollokoff) grew up in the Park Circle area (where Park Heights and Reisterstown Road meet), attended Isaac Davidson Hebrew School and became a Bar Mitzvah in Petach Tikvah Congregation. With theater on his mind and experience performing with the Alliance Players, he was able to break into television in the early 1950s as a part-time announcer on WAAM .

Between his career at WAAM (sold in 1957 by local owners Ben and Herman Cohen to Westinghouse to become WJZ) and WBAL-TV, Royal Parker seemed to be everywhere on the growing number of black-and-white television screens in Baltimore households. He has been an announcer, reporter, sports commentator and entertainer. "Over my forty years in Baltimore television, I did it all," says Mr. Parker.

But Royal Parker is best remembered for the children's character roles he took on in several shows. He was "Mr. PopLolly," a clown; "Big Pud" on the *Popeye* cartoon show; and "P.W. Doodle," a "newsboy" and host on the popular Mickey Mouse shows.

Jay Grayson (Goldberg) was best known as the host of WBAL-TV's *Date to Dance*. He grew up in Northwest Baltimore on Ocala Avenue, just below Park Circle and was, with his family, a member of Har Sinai Congregation. His show was quiet and relaxed. *Date to Dance* was actually a dance contest, featuring the slow and more graceful dancing of the over-forty set. Grayson, for this show, inexplicably insisted on wearing glasses with no lenses in them.

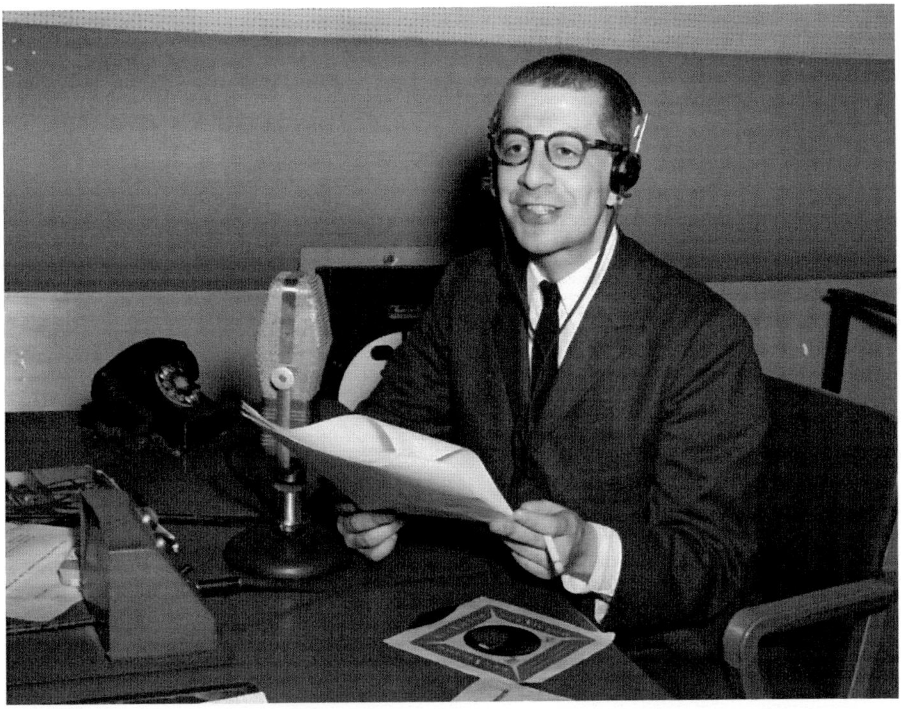

Jay Grayson, in his signature lens-less glasses, smiles for the camera behind his WBAL desk on December 15, 1959. *Courtesy of the University of Maryland Special Collections, Baltimore News American Collection and Hearst Corporation, CP 4.2012.9.*

Danny Sheelds (Gordon Shalowitz) was a product of the neighborhood around the Avalon Theater, on Santa Fe Avenue, a dead-end street that backed into the 4100 block of Park Heights Avenue. He started his showbiz career as a stand-up comic, so his style on television ran to the comic. He was forever reminding his viewers that his name was spelled with two e's ("Two eee's if you please!"). He is best remembered as master of ceremonies on what was a televised bingo show.

Other local Jewish television personalities who came into the picture in subsequent years include Richard Sher, Andy Barth, Marty Bass, Bob Turk, Deborah Weiner and Rich Hollander. There will be others in the years to come.

As for anti-Semitism in local television, Royal Parker says, "There was never any problem with a Jewish presence on camera here. In the 1950s, my own children taped a rendering of the Chanukah blessings, and the episode was shown on WAAM. And year after year, the rabbi of the Rogers Avenue Synagogue produced a show to celebrate every Jewish holiday. And it all seemed to belong, quite naturally." Rhea Feikin recalls, "I never felt that my being Jewish was ever a problem. It's true that there were no Jewish presidents of the stations, but that didn't seem to matter. Brent Gunts, president of WBAL-TV, cultivated diversity." Royal Parker sums up his experience: "The depiction of anti-Semitism may have been true in national network TV, but it certainly wasn't true in Baltimore TV. I was on-camera on Baltimore television for more than forty years, working for two different stations and I knew everyone at all of them. Anti-Semitism in Baltimore television? It never was."

Originally published as "Golden Age," March 26, 2004.

For Further Reading

On Jewish Baltimore

Argersinger, Joann E. *Making the Amalgamated: Gender, Ethnicity, and Class in the Baltimore Clothing Industry, 1899–1939*. Baltimore: Johns Hopkins University Press, 1999.

Decter, Avi Y., and Karen Falk, eds. *Of Hats and Harmonies: The Recollections of Baltimore's Lester S. Levy*. Baltimore: Jewish Museum of Maryland, 2005.

Decter, Avi Y., and Melissa Martens, eds. *Enterprising Emporiums: The Jewish Department Stores of Downtown Baltimore*. Baltimore: Jewish Museum of Maryland, 2001.

Decter, Avi Y., Anita Kassof and Deborah R. Weiner, eds. *Voices of Lombard Street: A Century of Change in East Baltimore*. Baltimore: Jewish Museum of Maryland, 2007.

Fein, Isaac M. *The Making of an American Jewish Community: The History of Baltimore Jewry from 1773 to 1920*. Philadelphia: Jewish Publication Society of America, 1971.

Jewish Museum of Maryland. "Telling Time: Stories and Storytellers in Honor of Gil Sandler." Themed issue of *Generations* magazine. Baltimore: Jewish Museum of Maryland, 2005/2006.

Kahn, Philip, Jr. *A Stitch in Time: The Four Seasons of Baltimore's Needle Trades*. Baltimore: Maryland Historical Society, 1989.

———. *Uncommon Threads: Threads That Wove the Fabric of Baltimore Jewish Life*. Baltimore: PECAN Publications, 1998.

Kessler, Barry. *Druid Hill Park: Jewish Baltimore's Green Oasis, 1920–1960.* Baltimore: Baltimore Jewish Environmental Network, 2009.

Lisicky, Michael J. *Hutzler's: Where Baltimore Shops.* Charleston, SC: The History Press, 2009.

Offit, Sidney. *Memoir of the Bookie's Son.* New York: St. Martin's Griffin, 1995.

Sandler, Gilbert. *Jewish Baltimore: A Family Album.* Baltimore: Johns Hopkins University Press, 2000.

Silberman, Lauren. *The Jewish Community of Baltimore.* Charleston, SC: Arcadia Publishing, 2008.

Silverman, Chip. *Diner Guys.* New York: Birch Lane Press, 1989.

On Baltimore

Olesker, Michael. *The Colts' Baltimore: A City and Its Love Affair in the 1950s.* Baltimore: Johns Hopkins University Press, 2008.

———. *Journeys to the Heart of Baltimore.* Baltimore: Johns Hopkins University Press, 2001.

Pietila, Antero. *Not in My Neighborhood: How Bigotry Shaped a Great American City.* Chicago: Ivan R. Dee, 2010.

Sandler, Gilbert. *Home Front Baltimore: An Album of Stories from World War II.* Baltimore: Johns Hopkins University Press, 2011.

———. *Small Town Baltimore: An Album of Memories.* Baltimore: Johns Hopkins University Press, 2001.

About the Author

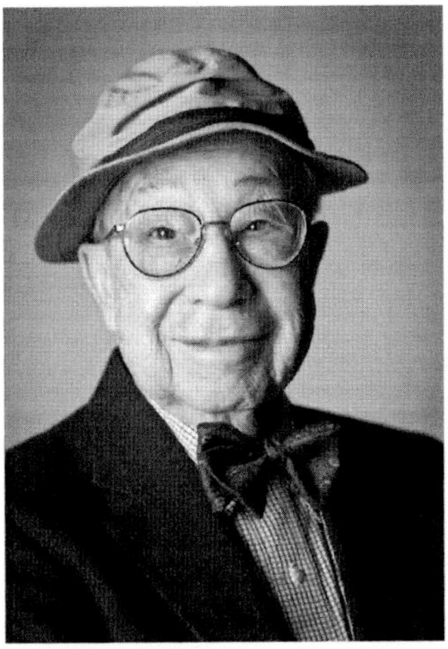

Photo by Skip Klein.

Gilbert Sandler is one of Baltimore's most-read and well-known local historians. For more than thirty years, through his articles in the *Baltimore Sun*, the *Baltimore Jewish Times*, National Public Radio and his books and lectures, he has shown Baltimoreans, through anecdote and memory, who they are, where they have been and, perhaps, where they are going. He was educated in Baltimore's public schools and graduated from Baltimore City College; in World War II, he served in the United States Navy as a ship-board navigator in the Pacific. He is a graduate of the University of Pennsylvania and has a master's from Johns Hopkins. He has been active, as he puts it, "Boy and man!" in Baltimore's Jewish community and admits that his involvement has provided him with the interest and curiosity to search out the stories that make up Jewish Baltimore.